THE TOUCHABLES ©

by KENT GAMBLE

THE TOUCHABLES ©

by KENT GAMBLE

Binary
PUBLICATIONS

BOOK EDITOR:
Gary Reed

PRODUCTION:
Dan Royer

www.binarypublications.com   email: binarypublications@gmail.com

WANTED

MR. BIG

4' 2" TALL   93 LBS.

WANTED FOR LEADING THE MOST BUMBLING GROUP OF MOBSTERS IN GANGLAND HISTORY. ALSO WANTED FOR CONSPIRACY TO EVOKE LAUGHTER.

WANTED

'FAST' EDDIE

5'5" TALL 106 LBS.

WANTED FOR POSING AS MR. BIG'S RIGHT-HAND MAN. HE IS AN INEPT WIMP'S WIMP. ALSO WANTED FOR BEING A CHRONIC UNDER-ACHIEVER AND LOSER.

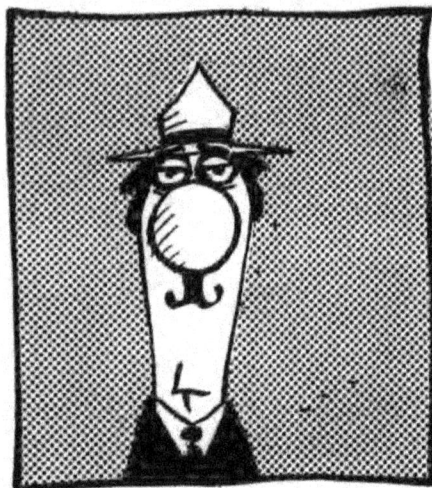

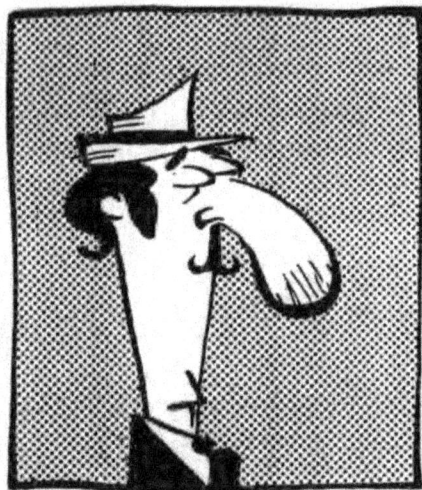

WANTED

THE BOYS

6' 6" TALL (EA)   286 LBS. (EA)

WANTED FOR CONSORTING WITH MR. BIG. A SORDID COLLECTION OF LOSERS, MISFITS AND MALCONTENTS. ALSO WANTED FOR IMPERSONATING A CROWD.

WANTED

MRS. BIG
5'3" TALL   166 LBS.

WANTED FOR PLAYING HOUSE WITH MR. BIG. THE GAME IS PLAYED ACCORDING TO HER RULES. ALSO WANTED FOR NAGGING, BROWBEATING AND HENPECKING.

WANTED

MR. GRAFT
5'7" TALL   176 LBS.

WANTED FOR ACTING AS MR. BIG'S MOUTHPIECE. KNOWN AS A LEGAL CONTORTIONIST, HE BENDS THE LAW COMPLETELY OUT OF SHAPE. ALSO WANTED FOR CONTEMPT OF COMEDY.

THE TOUCHABLES ©

BY KENT GAMBLE

BIG'S ARCH-ENEMY: 'FINGERS FOGERTY' AND COMPANY...

FOGERTY! BIG HERE!

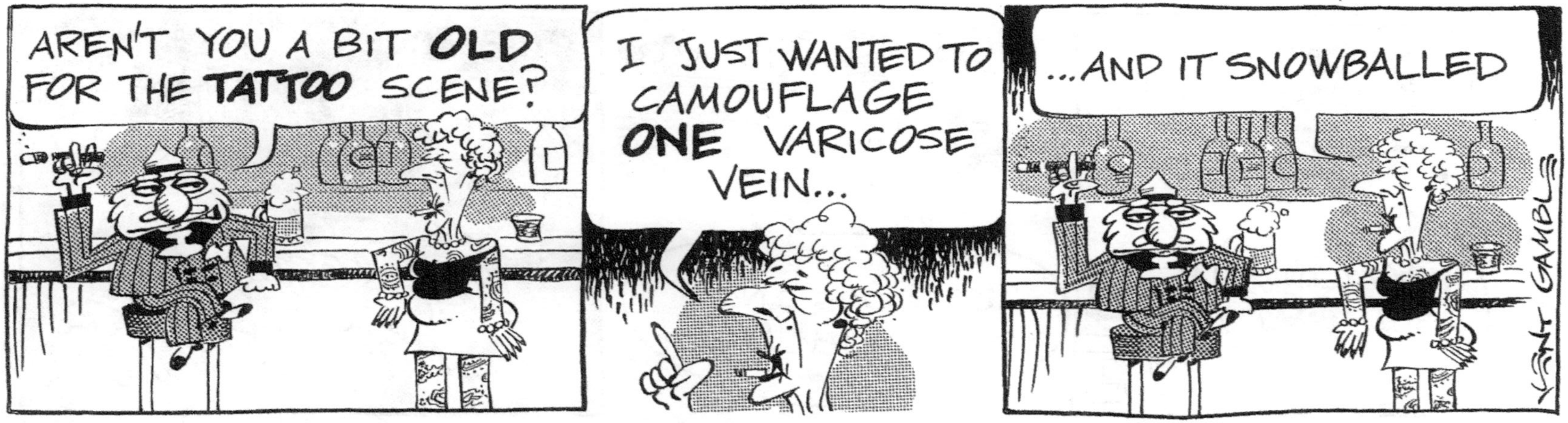
ARE'N'T YOU A BIT **OLD** FOR THE **TATTOO** SCENE?
I JUST WANTED TO CAMOUFLAGE **ONE** VARICOSE VEIN...
...AND IT SNOWBALLED
KENT GAMBLE

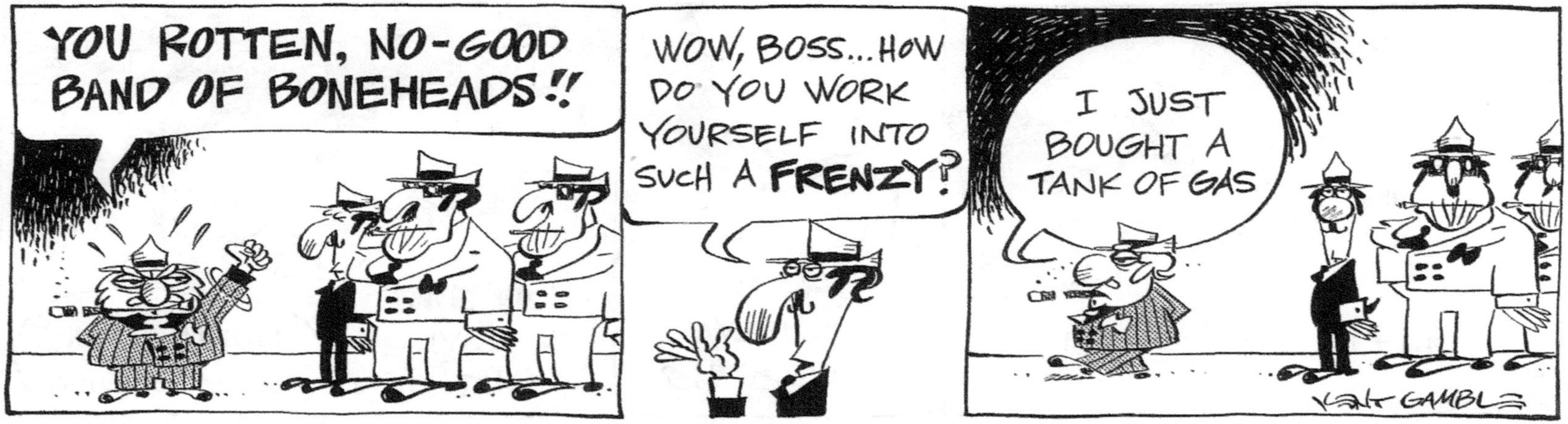
YOU ROTTEN, NO-GOOD BAND OF BONEHEADS!!
WOW, BOSS...HOW DO YOU WORK YOURSELF INTO SUCH A **FRENZY**?
I JUST BOUGHT A TANK OF GAS
KENT GAMBLE

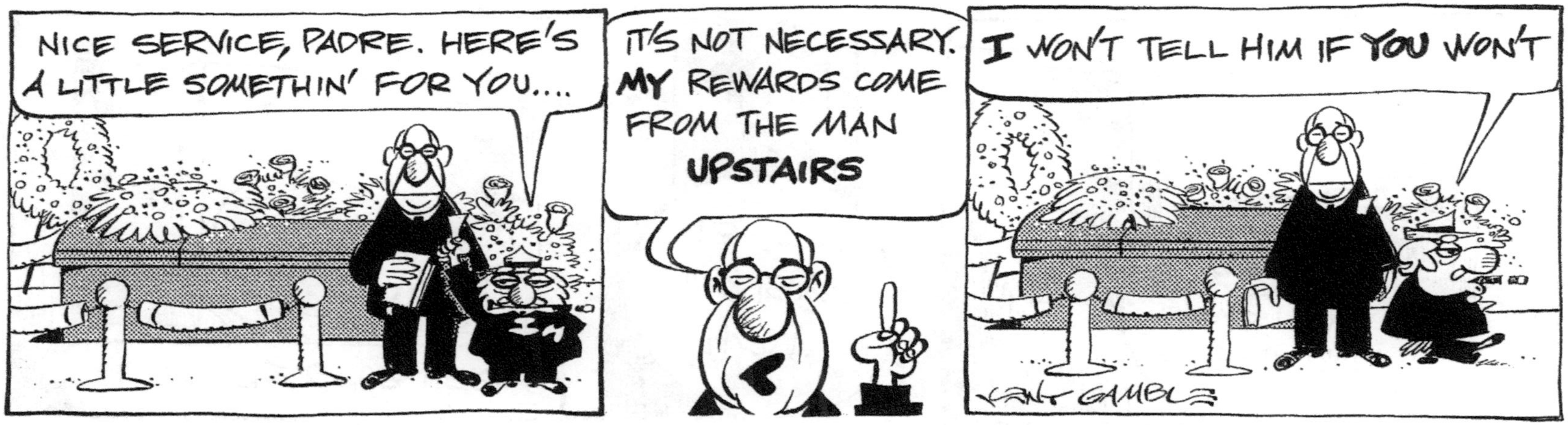
NICE SERVICE, PADRE. HERE'S A LITTLE SOMETHIN' FOR YOU....
IT'S NOT NECESSARY. **MY** REWARDS COME FROM THE MAN **UPSTAIRS**
I WON'T TELL HIM IF **YOU** WON'T
KENT GAMBLE

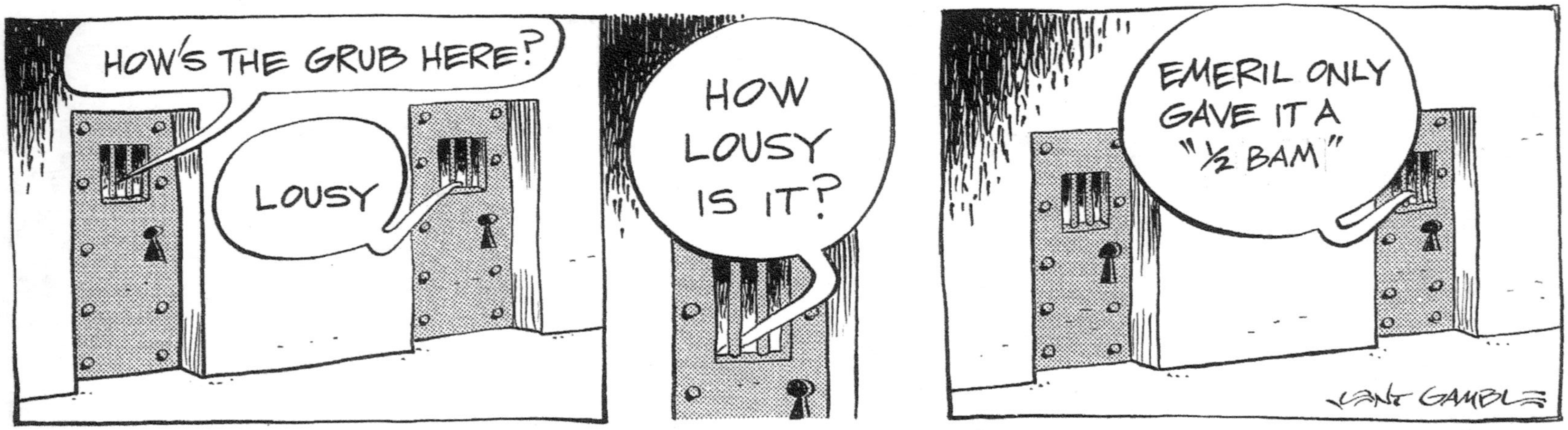
HOW'S THE GRUB HERE?
LOUSY
HOW LOUSY IS IT?
EMERIL ONLY GAVE IT A "½ BAM"
KENT GAMBLE

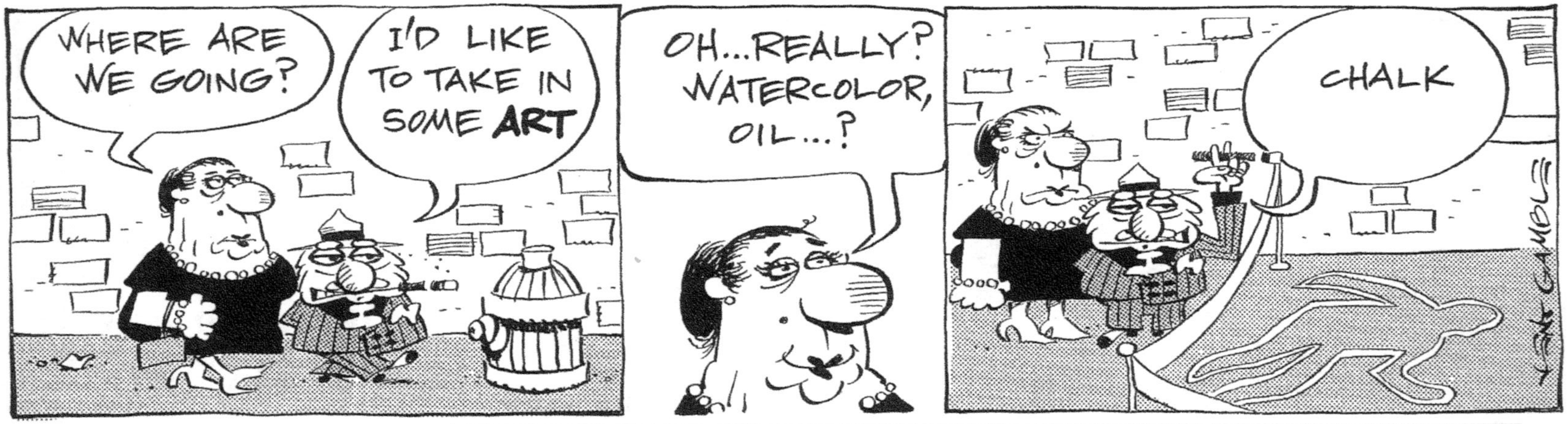
WHERE ARE WE GOING?
I'D LIKE TO TAKE IN SOME **ART**
OH... REALLY? WATERCOLOR, OIL...?
CHALK
KENT GAMBLE

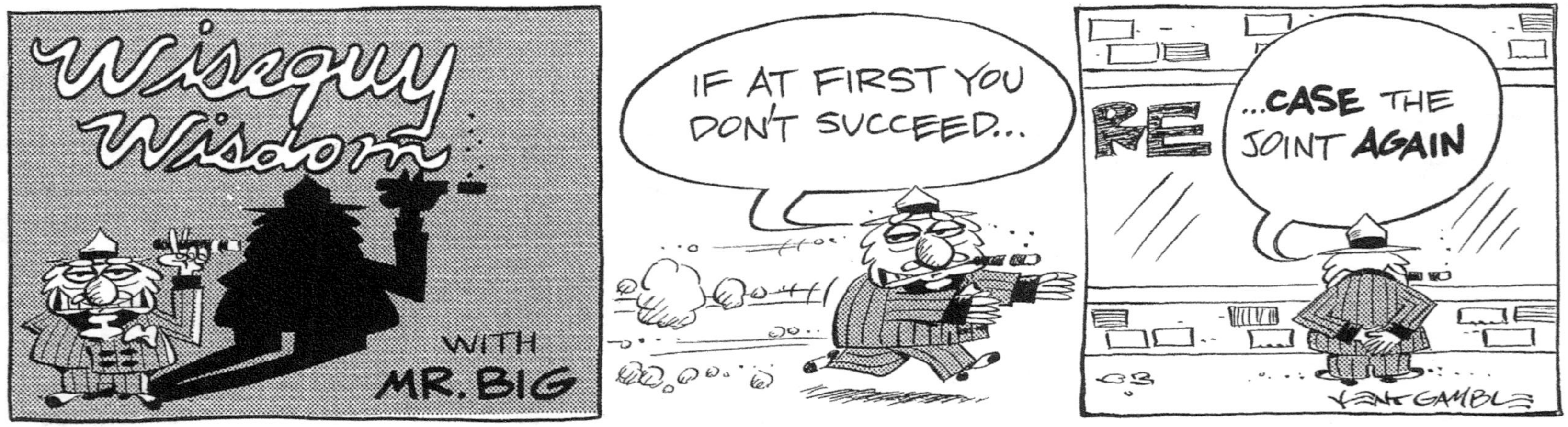
Wiseguy Wisdom
WITH MR. BIG
IF AT FIRST YOU DON'T SUCCEED...
RE
...**CASE** THE JOINT **AGAIN**
KENT GAMBLE

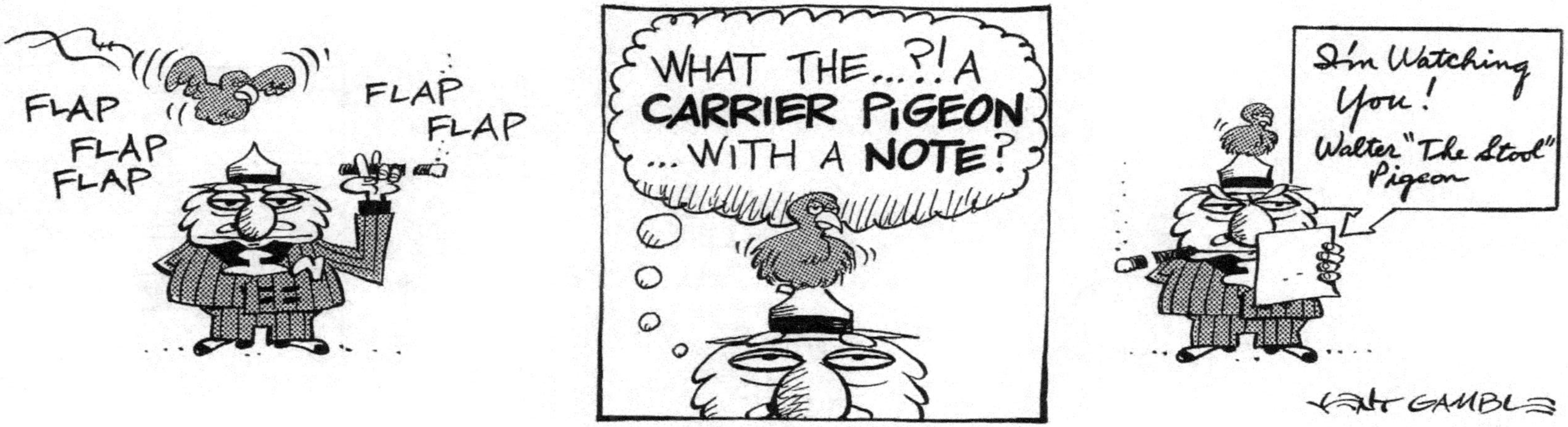
FLAP
FLAP
FLAP
FLAP
FLAP
WHAT THE...?! A CARRIER PIGEON ...WITH A NOTE?
I'm Watching You! Walter "The Stool" Pigeon
KENT GAMBLE

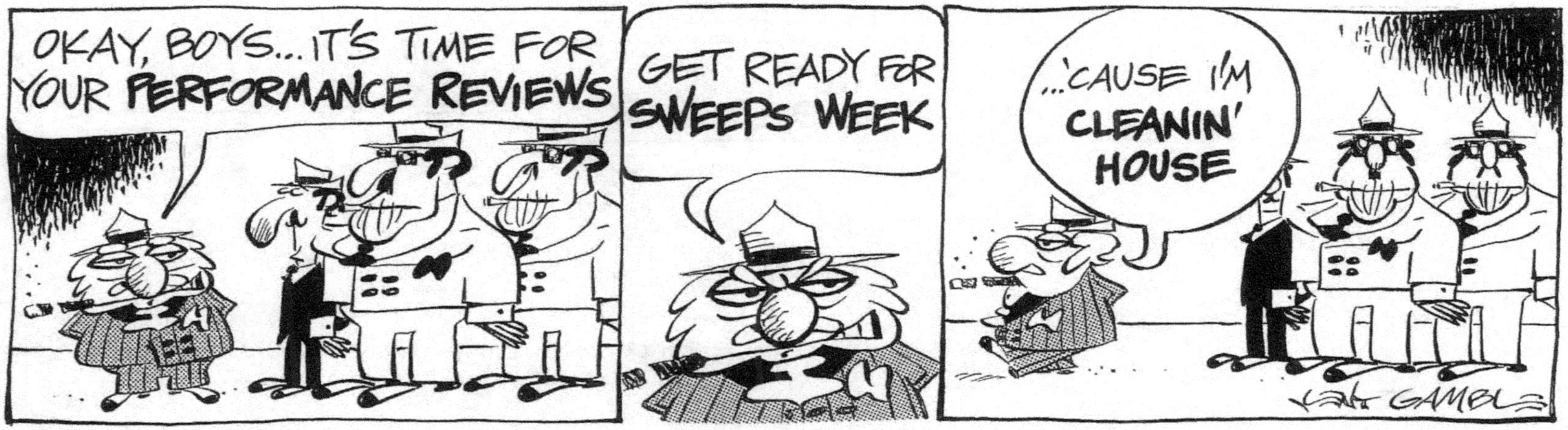
OKAY, BOYS... IT'S TIME FOR YOUR PERFORMANCE REVIEWS
GET READY FOR SWEEPS WEEK
...'CAUSE I'M CLEANIN' HOUSE
KENT GAMBLE

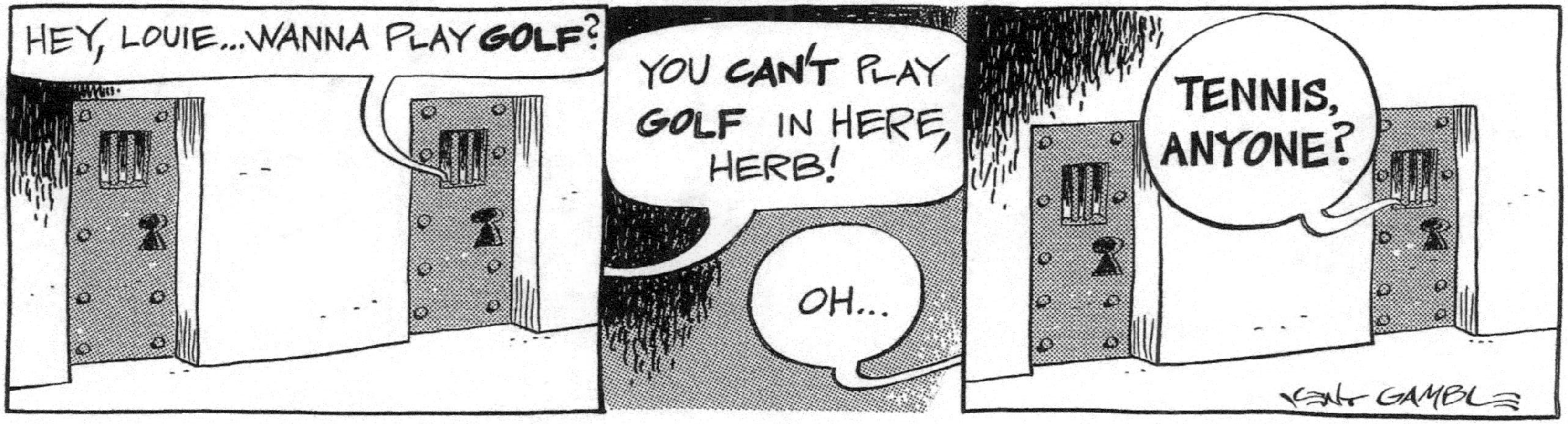
HEY, LOUIE...WANNA PLAY GOLF?
YOU CAN'T PLAY GOLF IN HERE, HERB!
OH...
TENNIS, ANYONE?
KENT GAMBLE

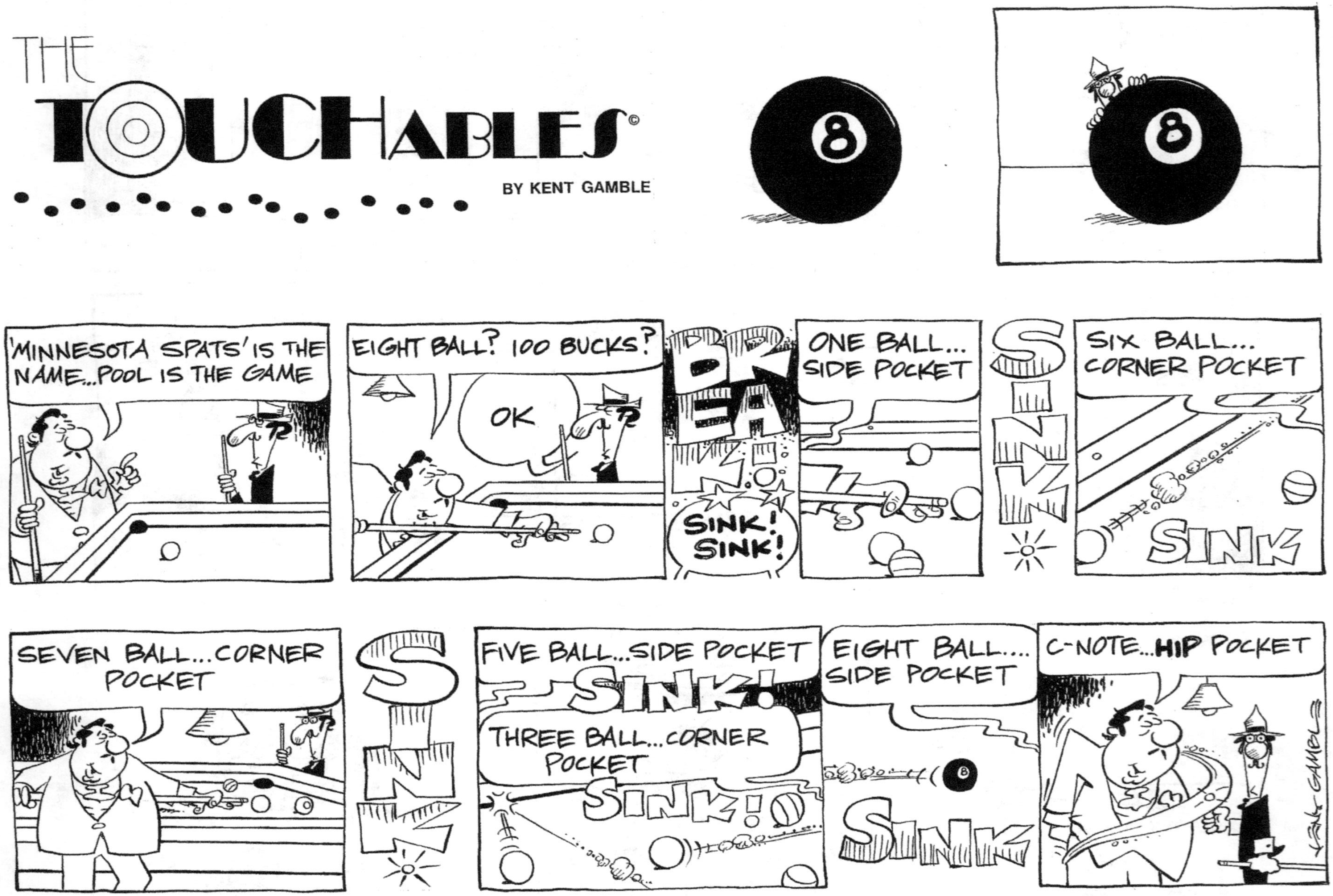
THE TOUCHABLES©
BY KENT GAMBLE
'MINNESOTA SPATS' IS THE NAME...POOL IS THE GAME
EIGHT BALL? 100 BUCKS?
OK
BREAK
SINK! SINK!
ONE BALL... SIDE POCKET
SINK
SIX BALL... CORNER POCKET
SINK
SEVEN BALL...CORNER POCKET
SINK
FIVE BALL...SIDE POCKET
SINK!
THREE BALL...CORNER POCKET
SINK!
EIGHT BALL.... SIDE POCKET
SINK
C-NOTE...HIP POCKET
KENT GAMBLE

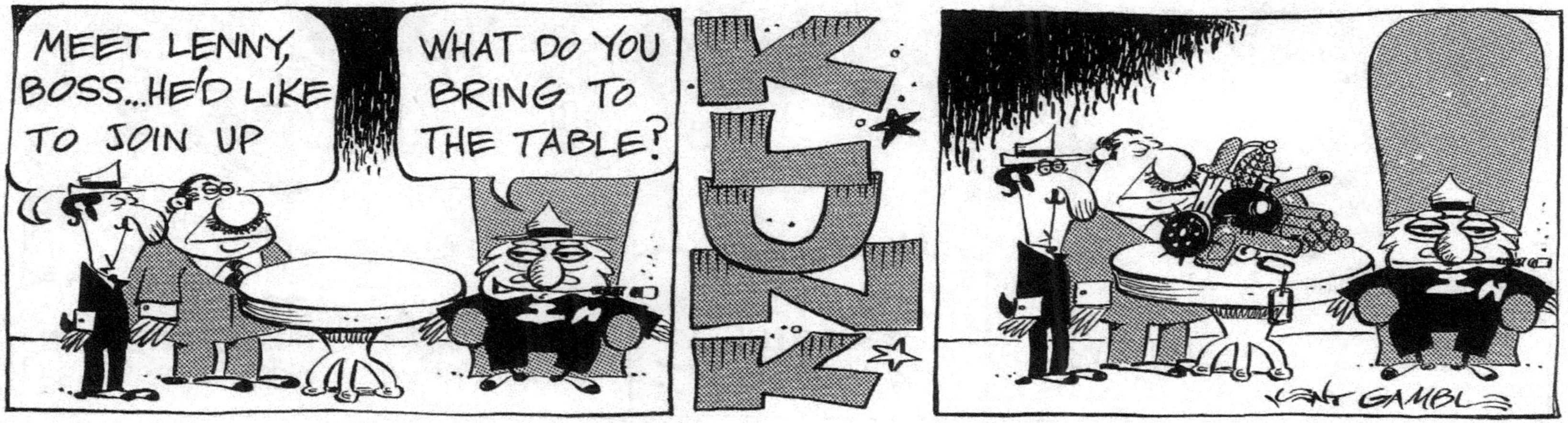
MEET LENNY, BOSS...HE'D LIKE TO JOIN UP
WHAT DO YOU BRING TO THE TABLE?
KLUNK
KENT GAMBLE

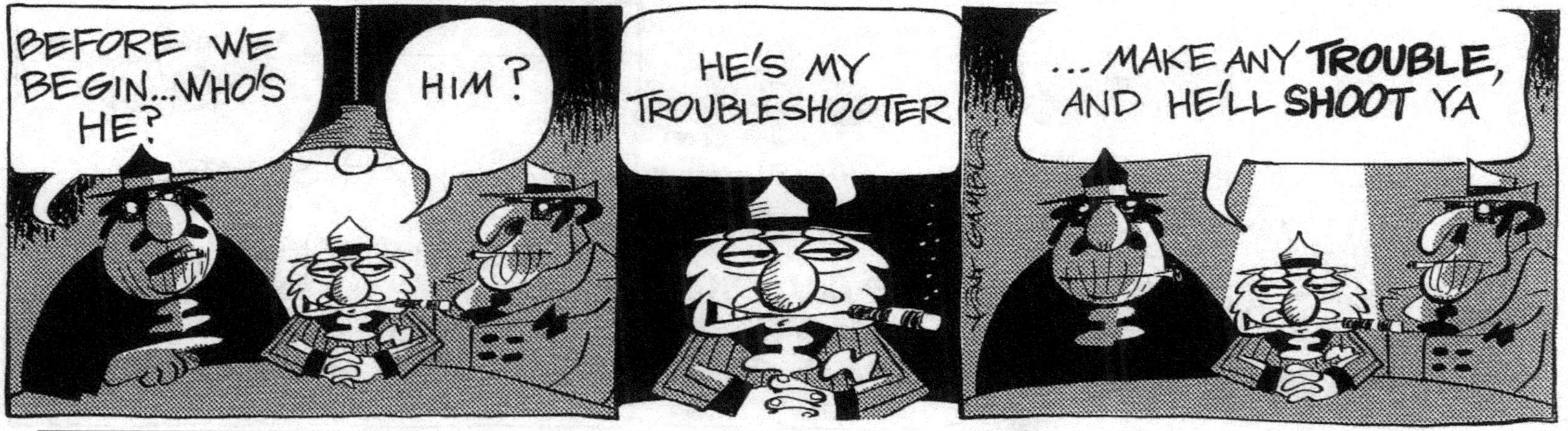
BEFORE WE BEGIN...WHO'S HE?
HIM?
HE'S MY TROUBLESHOOTER
... MAKE ANY **TROUBLE**, AND HE'LL **SHOOT** YA
KENT GAMBLE

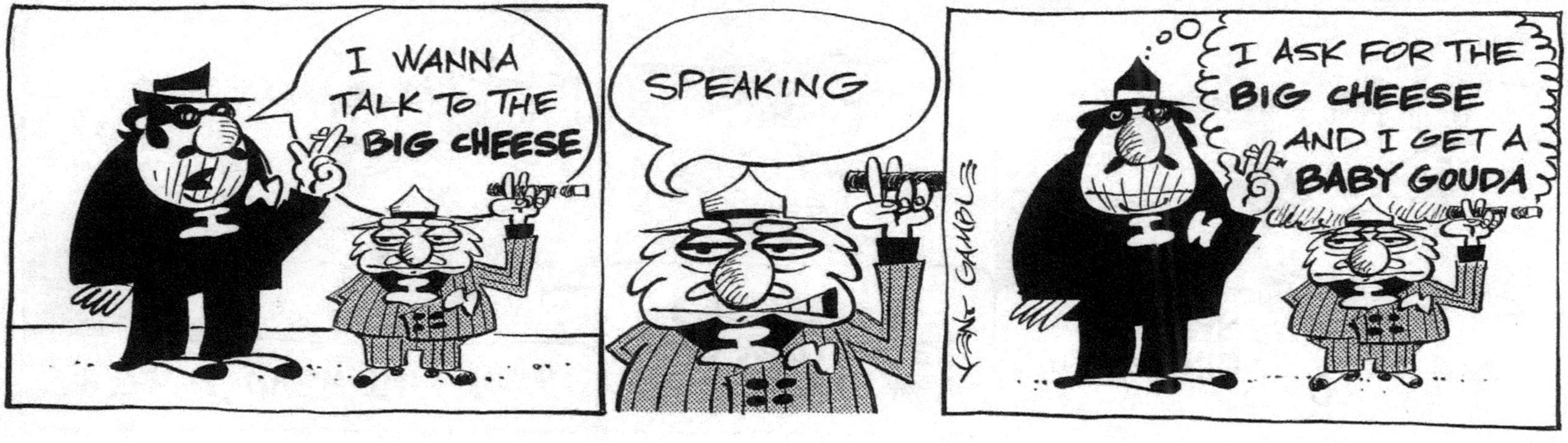
I WANNA TALK TO THE **BIG CHEESE**
SPEAKING
I ASK FOR THE **BIG CHEESE** AND I GET A **BABY GOUDA**
KENT GAMBLE

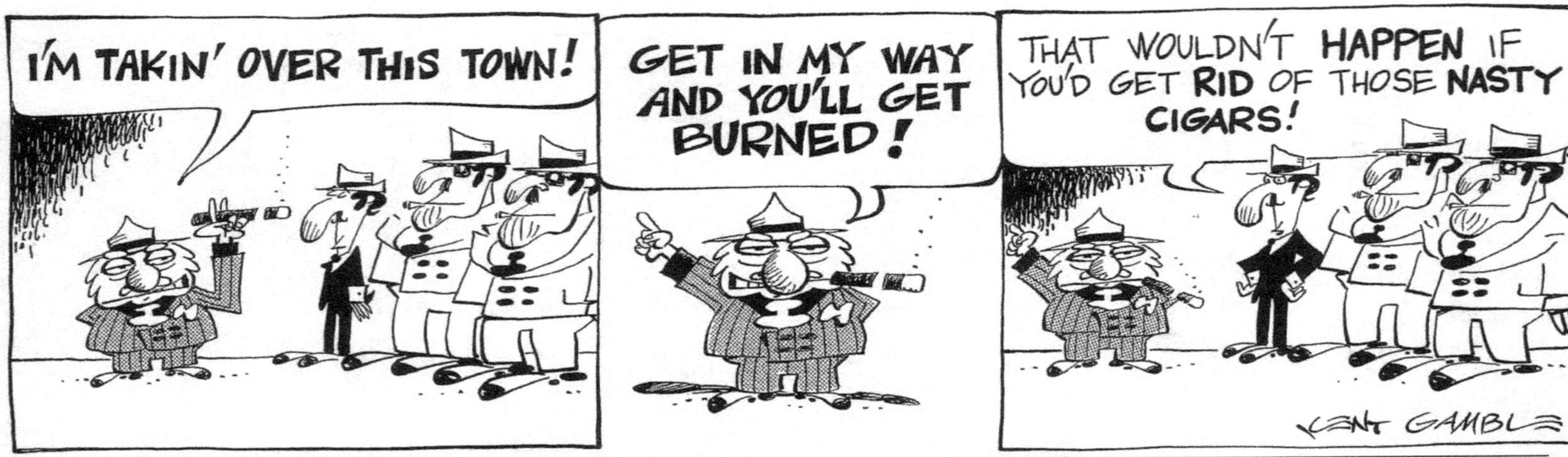
I'M TAKIN' OVER THIS TOWN!
GET IN MY WAY AND YOU'LL GET BURNED!
THAT WOULDN'T HAPPEN IF YOU'D GET RID OF THOSE NASTY CIGARS!
KENT GAMBLE

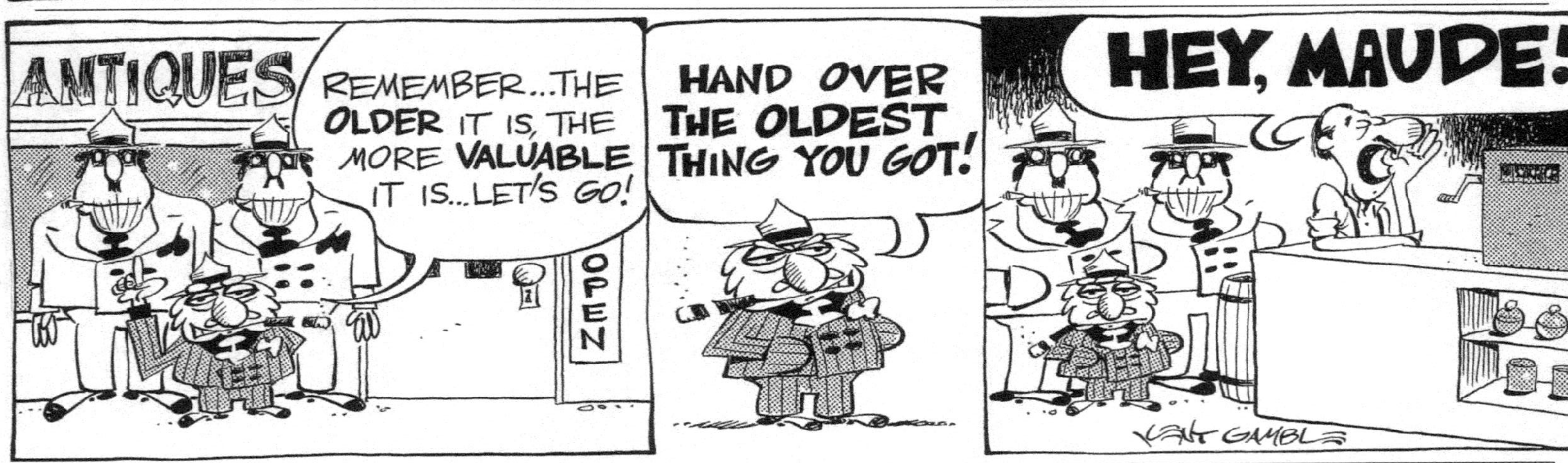
ANTIQUES
REMEMBER...THE OLDER IT IS, THE MORE VALUABLE IT IS...LET'S GO!
OPEN
HAND OVER THE OLDEST THING YOU GOT!
HEY, MAUDE!
KENT GAMBLE

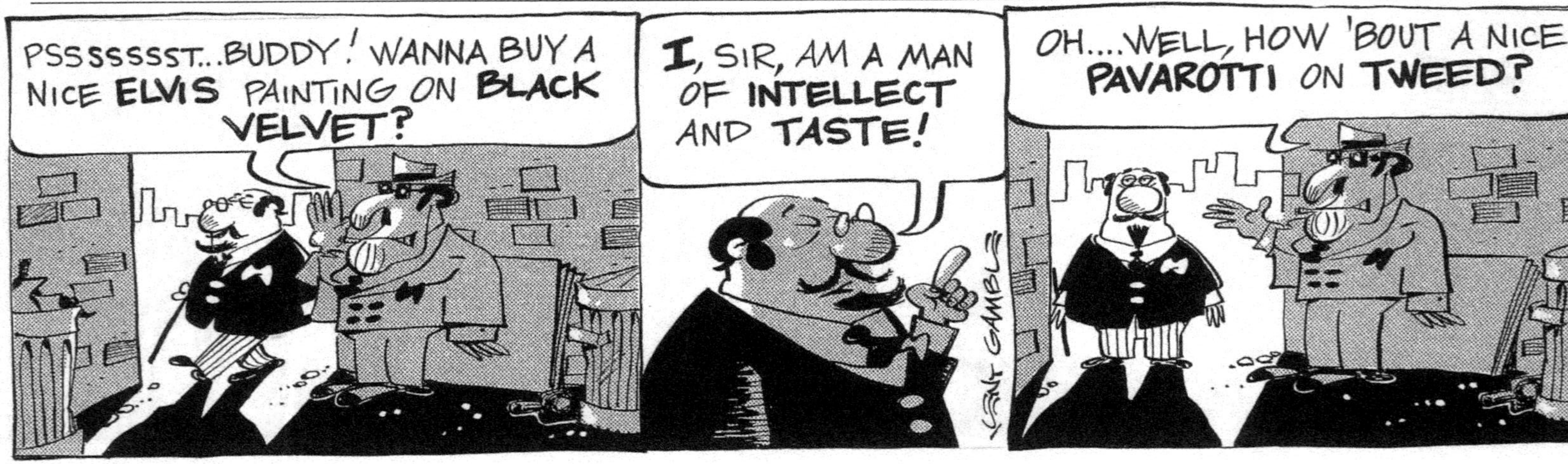
PSSSSSST...BUDDY! WANNA BUY A NICE ELVIS PAINTING ON BLACK VELVET?
I, SIR, AM A MAN OF INTELLECT AND TASTE!
KENT GAMBLE
OH....WELL, HOW 'BOUT A NICE PAVAROTTI ON TWEED?

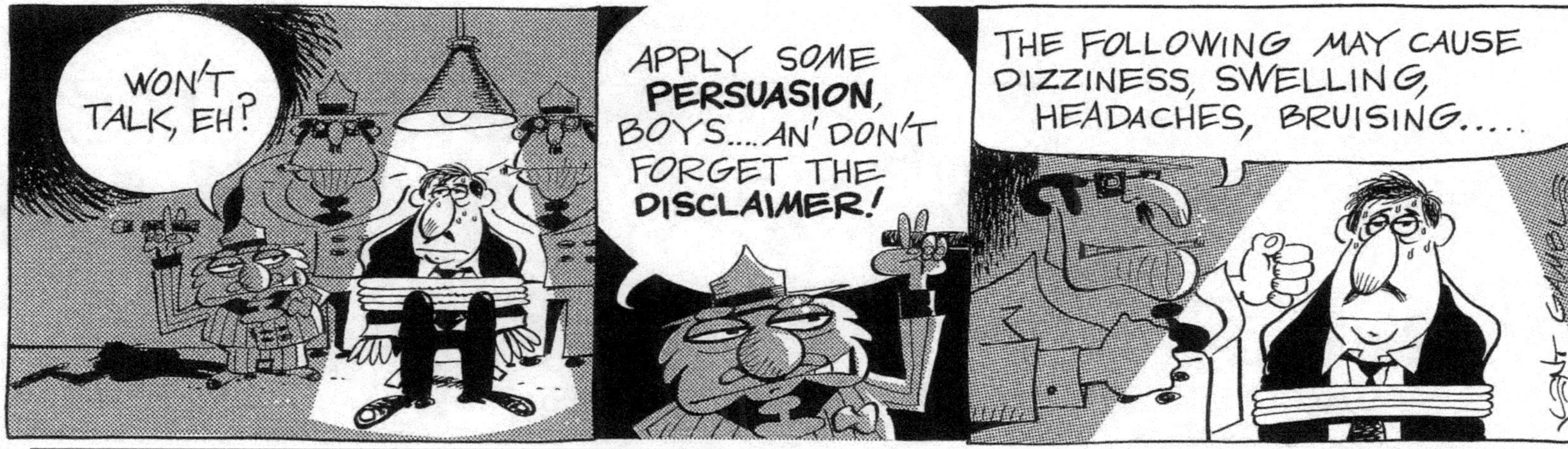
WON'T TALK, EH?
APPLY SOME **PERSUASION**, BOYS.... AN' DON'T FORGET THE **DISCLAIMER**!
THE FOLLOWING MAY CAUSE DIZZINESS, SWELLING, HEADACHES, BRUISING.....
KENT GAMBLE

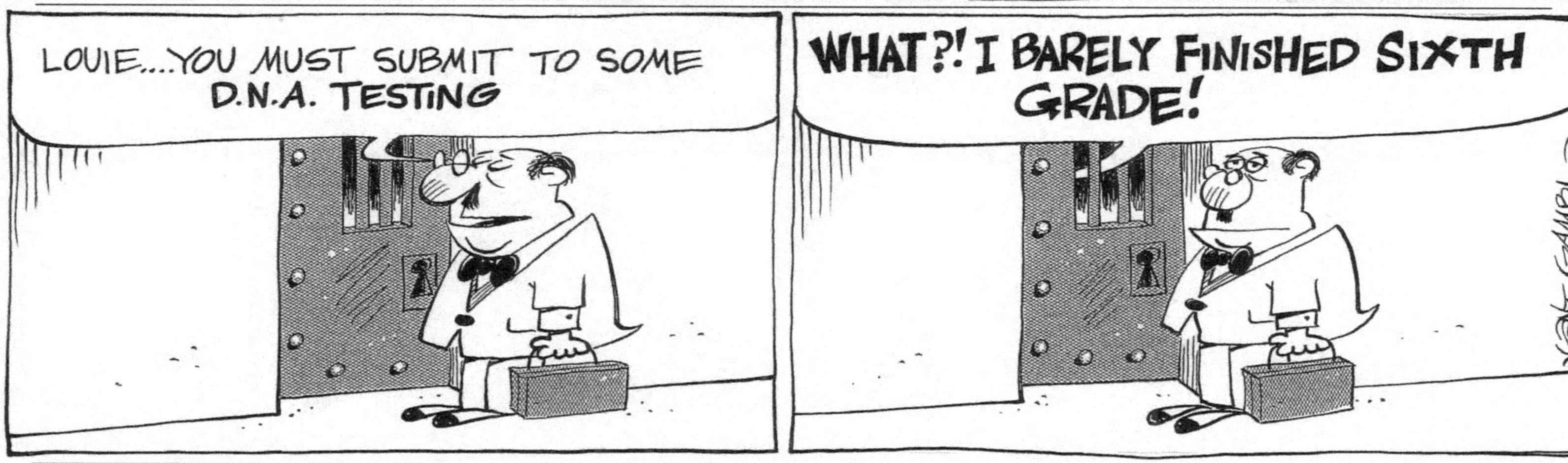
LOUIE.... YOU MUST SUBMIT TO SOME **D.N.A. TESTING**
WHAT?! I BARELY FINISHED SIXTH GRADE!
KENT GAMBLE

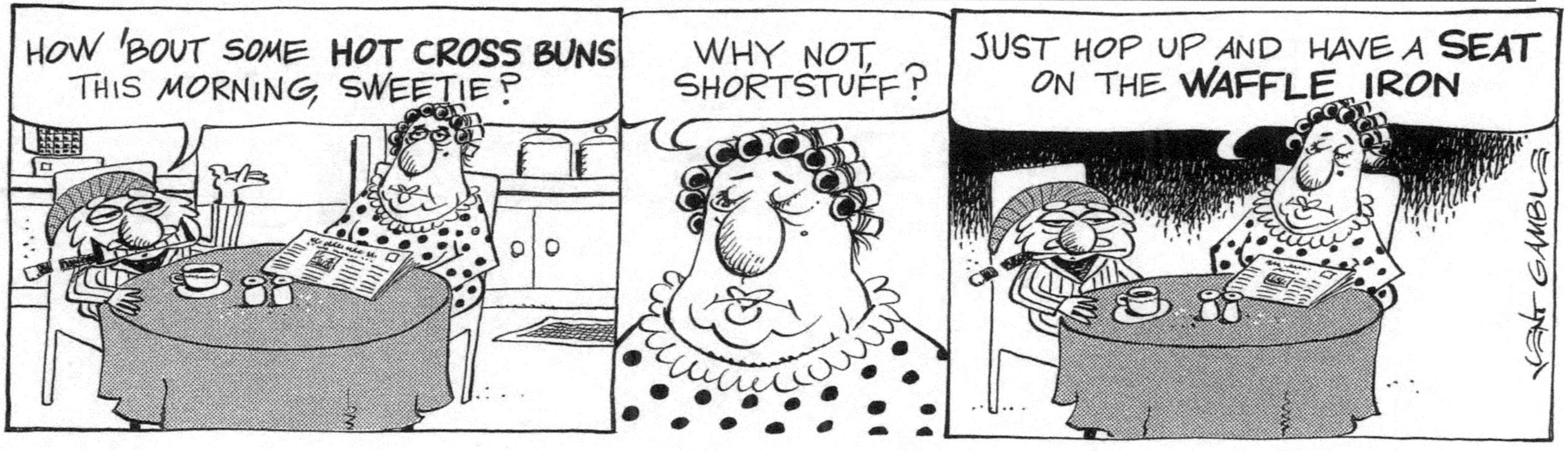
HOW 'BOUT SOME **HOT CROSS BUNS** THIS MORNING, SWEETIE?
WHY NOT, SHORTSTUFF?
JUST HOP UP AND HAVE A **SEAT** ON THE **WAFFLE IRON**
KENT GAMBLE

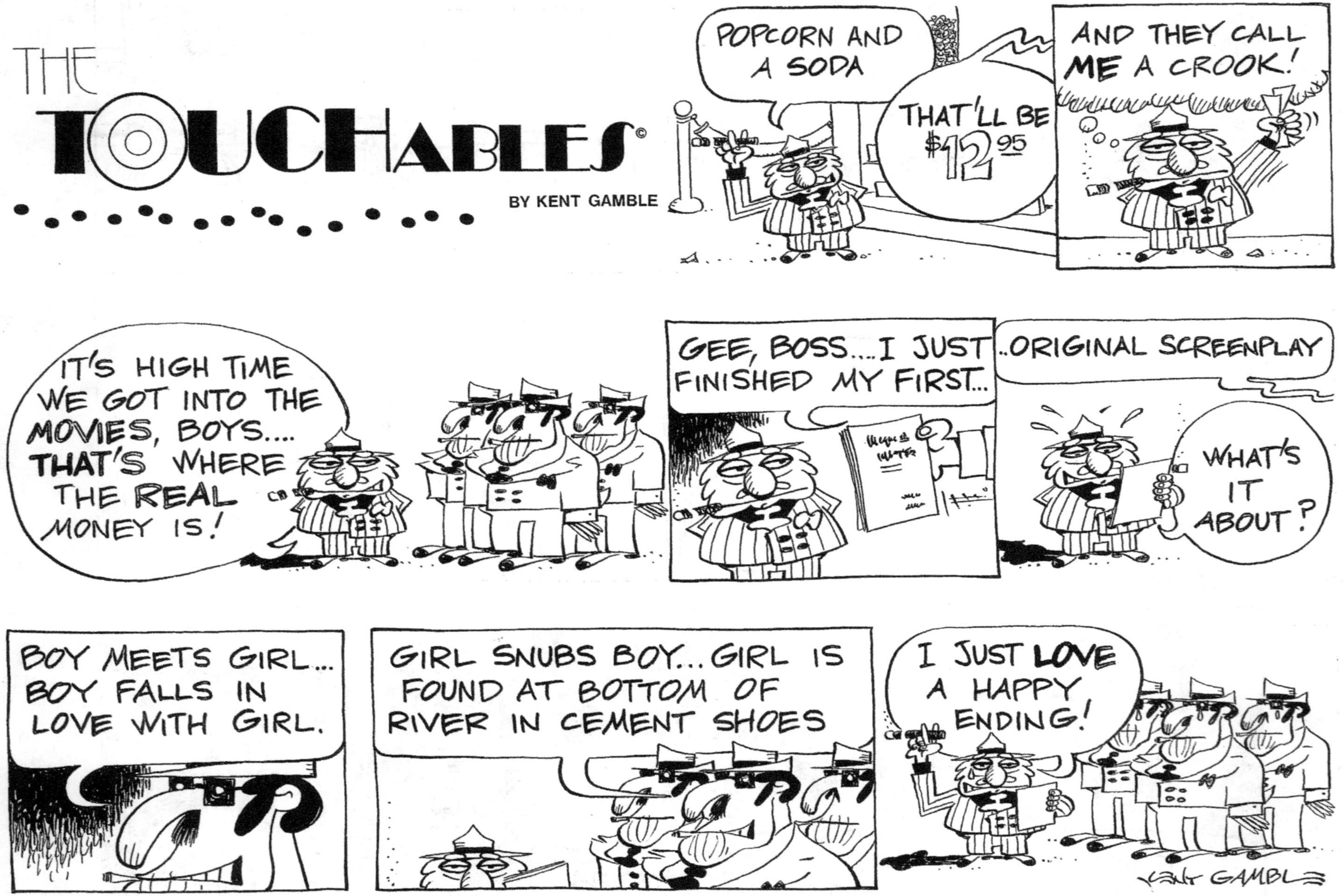
THE TOUCHABLES©
BY KENT GAMBLE
POPCORN AND A SODA
THAT'LL BE $12.95
AND THEY CALL ME A CROOK!
IT'S HIGH TIME WE GOT INTO THE MOVIES, BOYS.... THAT'S WHERE THE REAL MONEY IS!
GEE, BOSS.... I JUST FINISHED MY FIRST...
..ORIGINAL SCREENPLAY
WHAT'S IT ABOUT?
BOY MEETS GIRL... BOY FALLS IN LOVE WITH GIRL.
GIRL SNUBS BOY... GIRL IS FOUND AT BOTTOM OF RIVER IN CEMENT SHOES
I JUST LOVE A HAPPY ENDING!
KENT GAMBLE

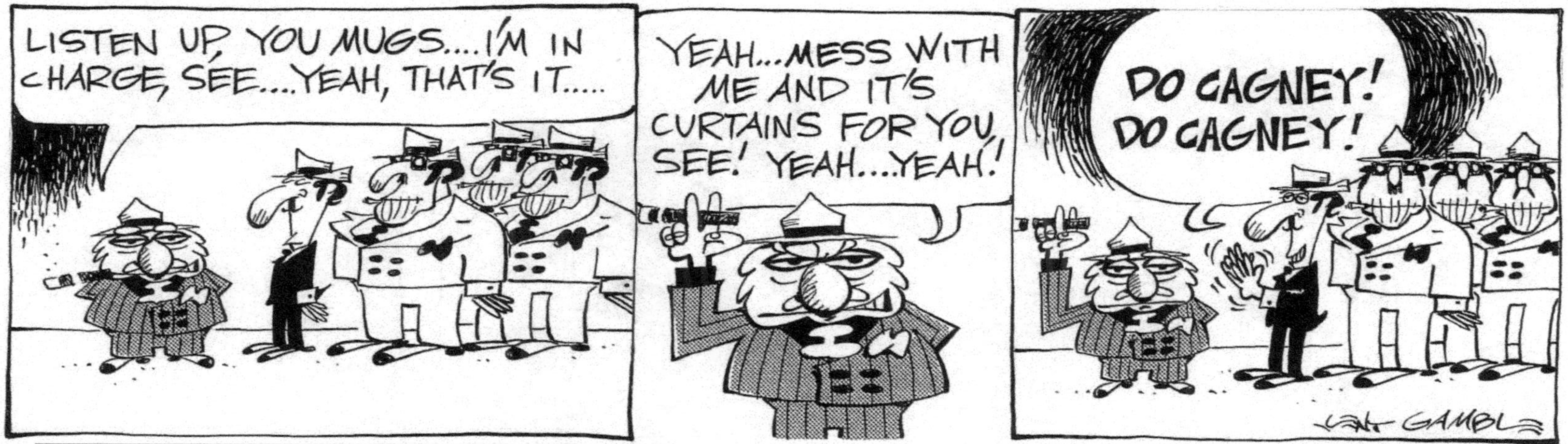
LISTEN UP, YOU MUGS.....I'M IN CHARGE, SEE....YEAH, THAT'S IT.....
YEAH...MESS WITH ME AND IT'S CURTAINS FOR YOU, SEE! YEAH....YEAH!
DO CAGNEY! DO CAGNEY!
KENT GAMBLE

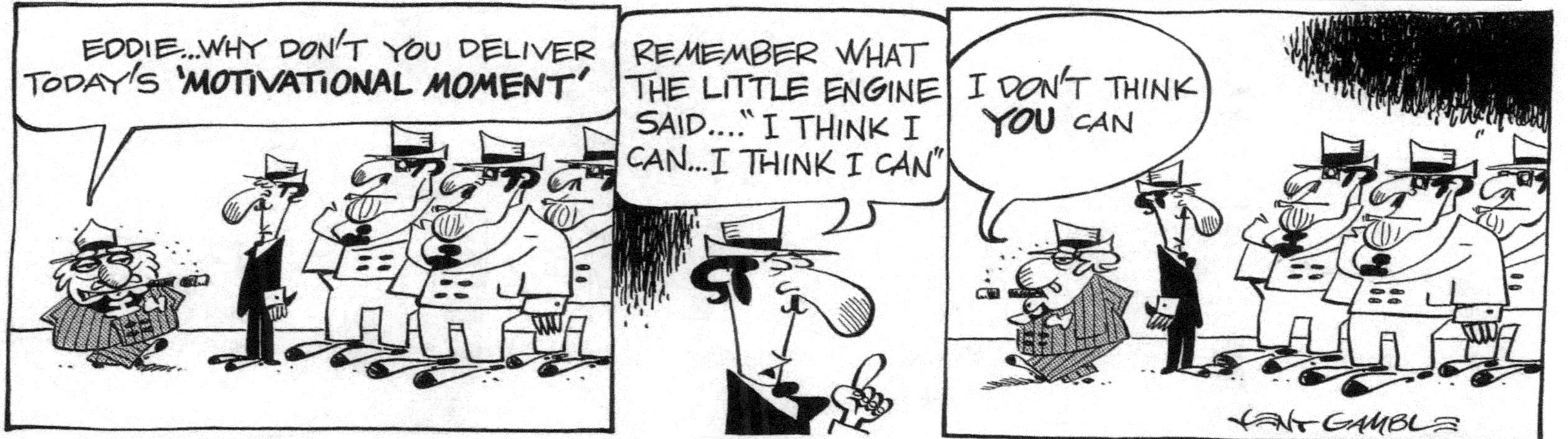
EDDIE...WHY DON'T YOU DELIVER TODAY'S 'MOTIVATIONAL MOMENT'
REMEMBER WHAT THE LITTLE ENGINE SAID...." I THINK I CAN...I THINK I CAN"
I DON'T THINK YOU CAN
KENT GAMBLE

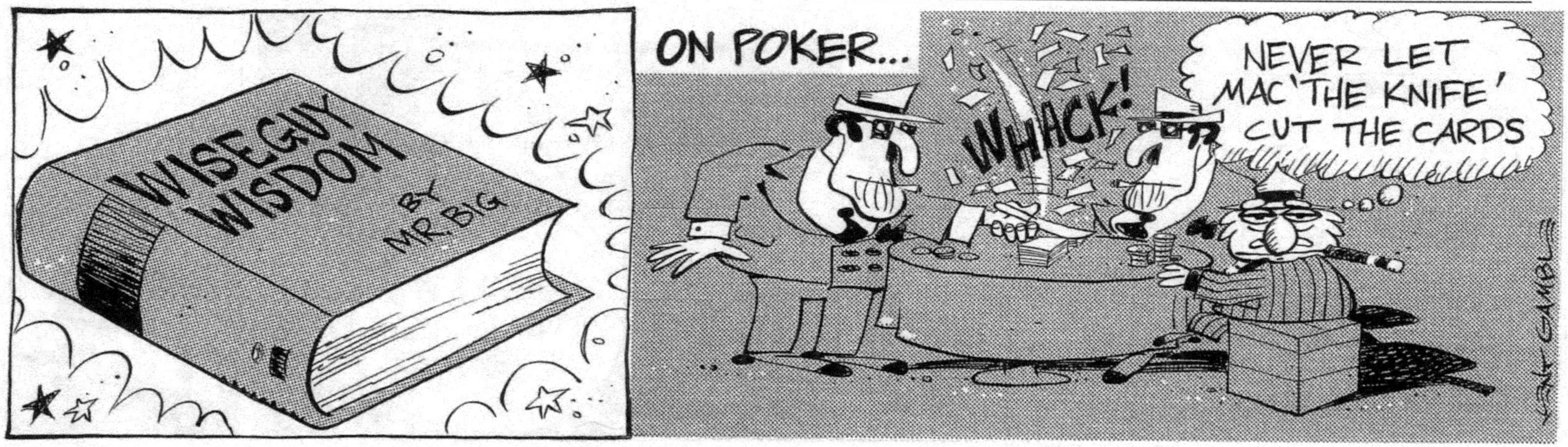
WISEGUY WISDOM
BY MR. BIG
ON POKER...
WHACK!
NEVER LET MAC 'THE KNIFE' CUT THE CARDS
KENT GAMBLE

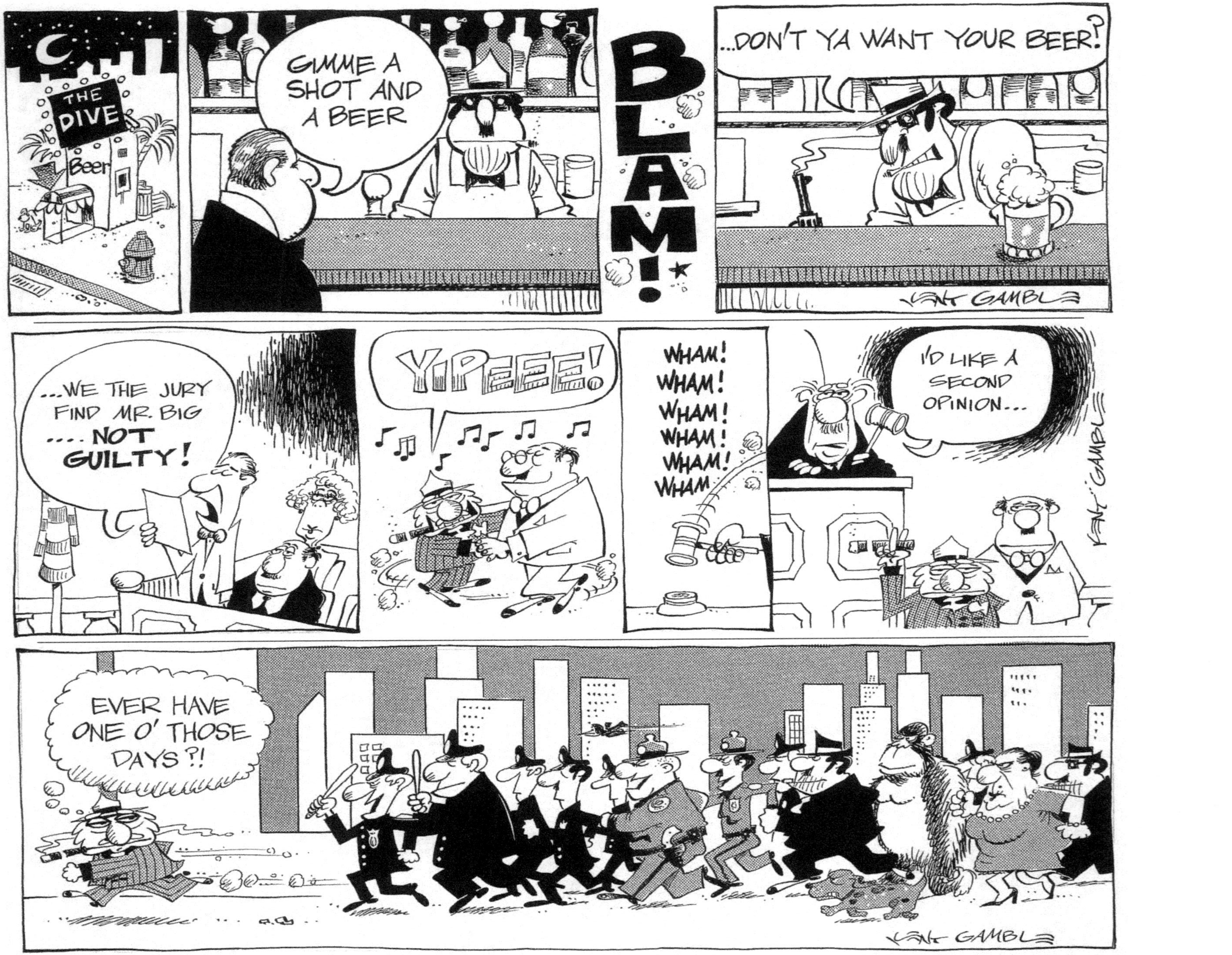
THE DIVE
Beer
GIMME A SHOT AND A BEER
BLAM!
...DON'T YA WANT YOUR BEER?
KENT GAMBLE
...WE THE JURY FIND MR. BIG .... NOT GUILTY!
YIPEEE!
WHAM! WHAM! WHAM! WHAM! WHAM! WHAM
I'D LIKE A SECOND OPINION...
KENT GAMBLE
EVER HAVE ONE O' THOSE DAYS?!
KENT GAMBLE

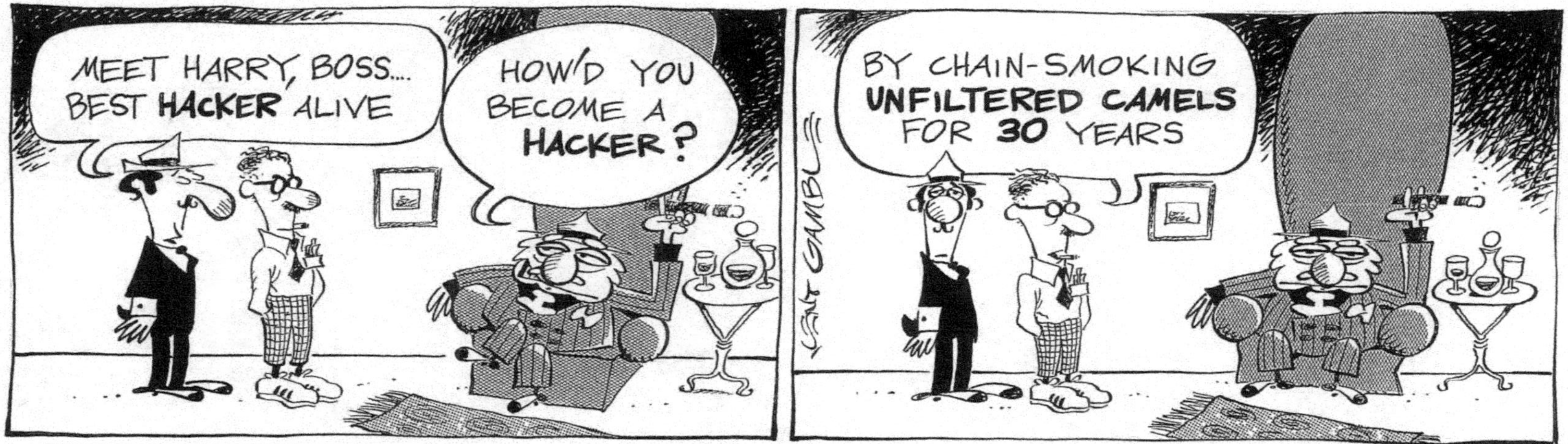
MEET HARRY, BOSS.... BEST **HACKER** ALIVE
HOW'D YOU BECOME A **HACKER**?
BY CHAIN-SMOKING **UNFILTERED CAMELS** FOR **30** YEARS

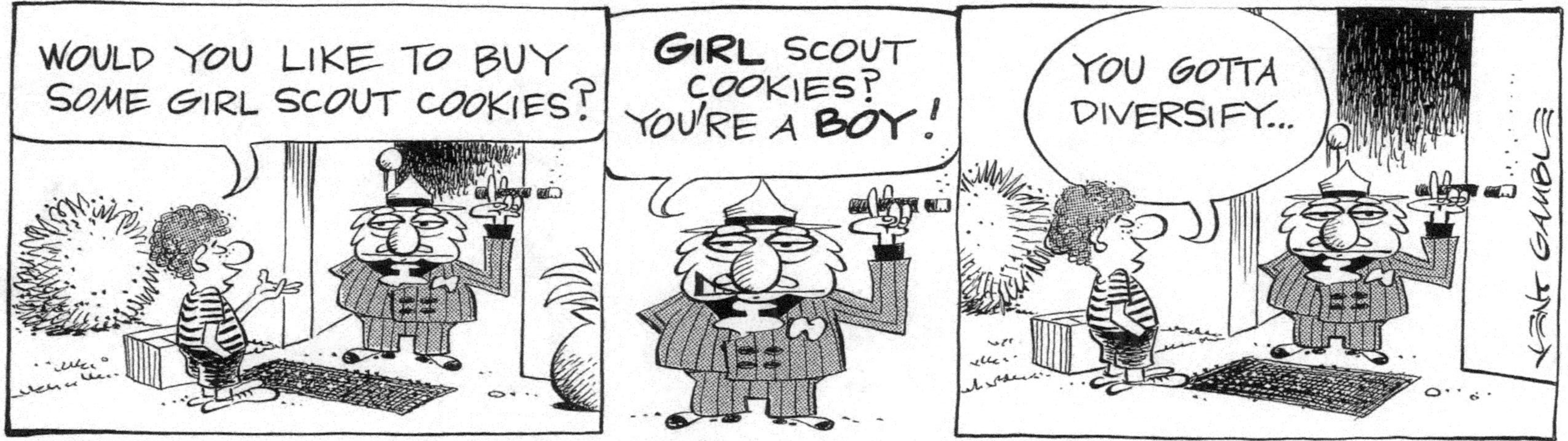
WOULD YOU LIKE TO BUY SOME GIRL SCOUT COOKIES?
GIRL SCOUT COOKIES? YOU'RE A **BOY**!
YOU GOTTA DIVERSIFY...

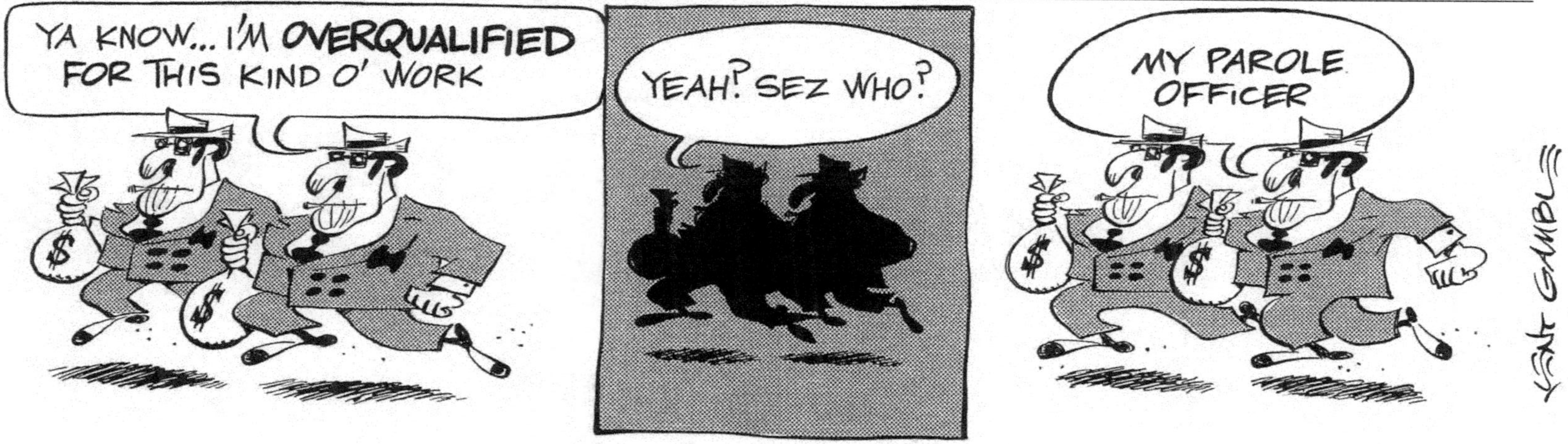
YA KNOW... I'M **OVERQUALIFIED** FOR THIS KIND O' WORK
YEAH? SEZ WHO?
MY PAROLE OFFICER

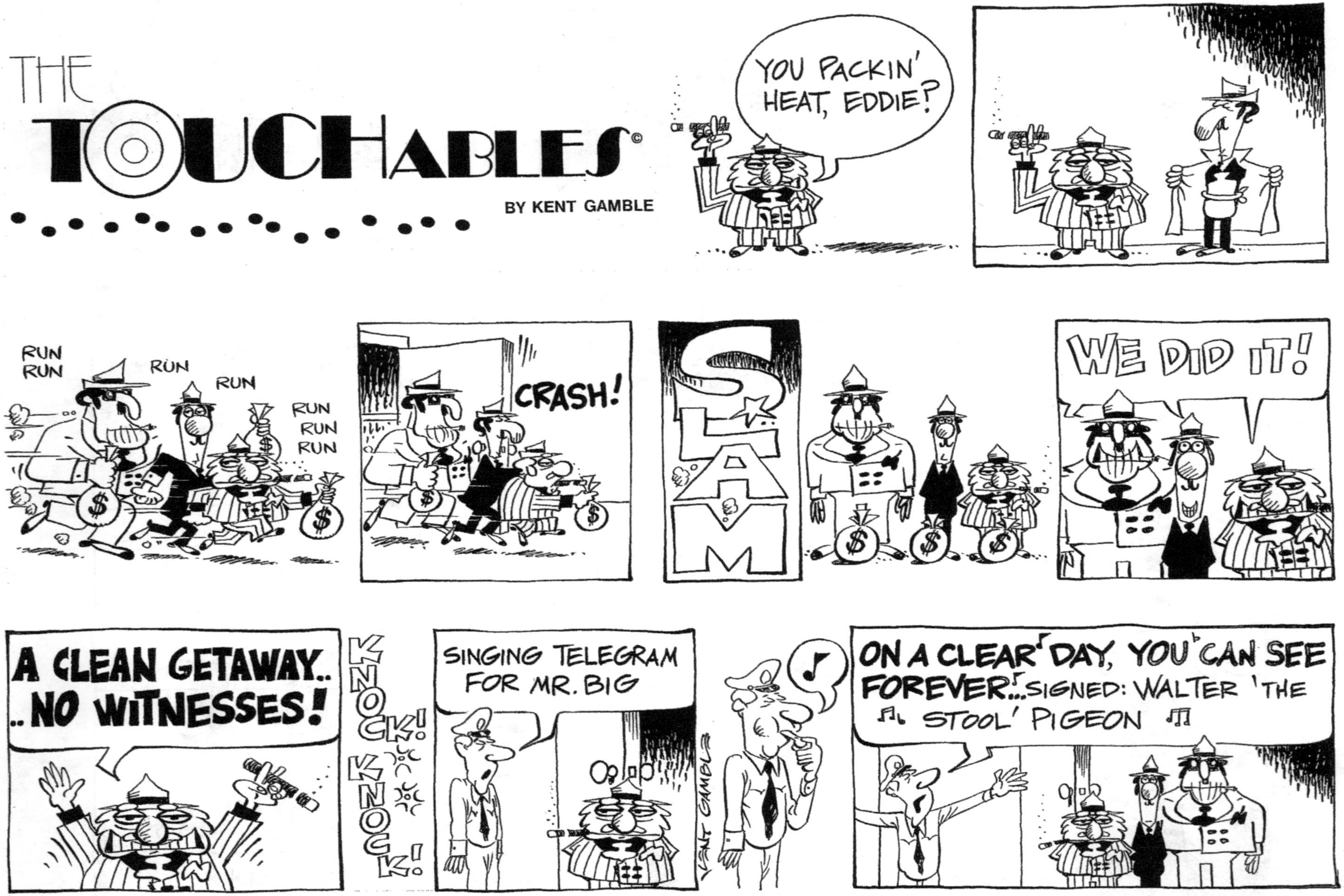
THE TOUCHABLES©
BY KENT GAMBLE
YOU PACKIN' HEAT, EDDIE?
RUN RUN
RUN
RUN
RUN RUN RUN
CRASH!
SLAM
WE DID IT!
A CLEAN GETAWAY.. ..NO WITNESSES!
KNOCK! KNOCK!
SINGING TELEGRAM FOR MR. BIG
KENT GAMBLE
ON A CLEAR DAY, YOU CAN SEE FOREVER!...SIGNED: WALTER 'THE STOOL' PIGEON

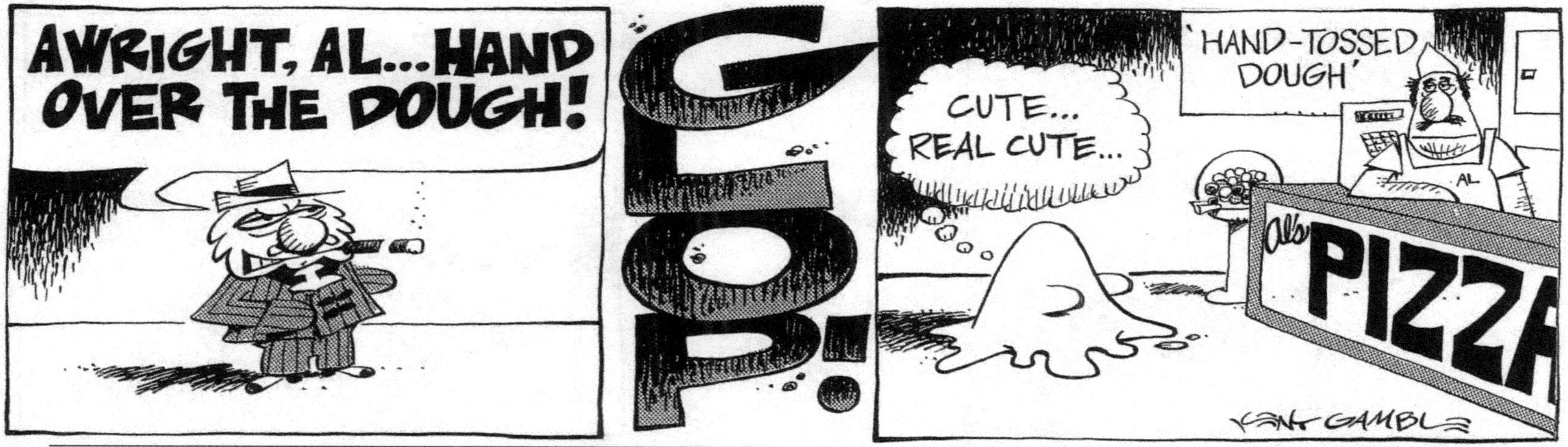
AWRIGHT, AL... HAND OVER THE DOUGH!
GLOP!
CUTE... REAL CUTE...
'HAND-TOSSED DOUGH'
AL
Al's PIZZA
KENT GAMBLE

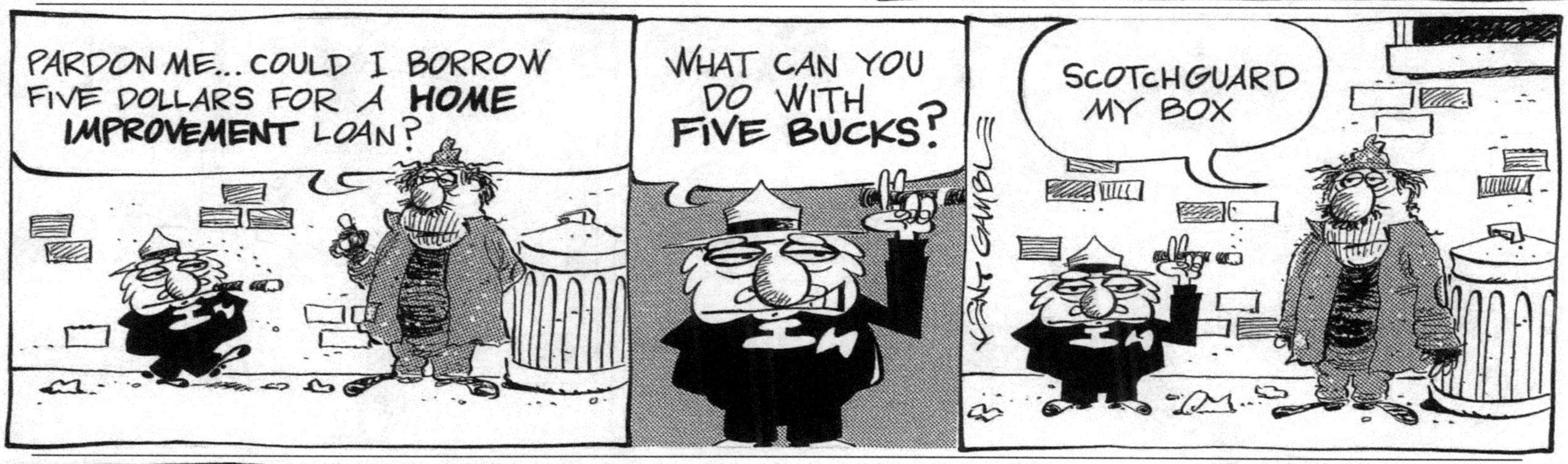
PARDON ME... COULD I BORROW FIVE DOLLARS FOR A HOME IMPROVEMENT LOAN?
WHAT CAN YOU DO WITH FIVE BUCKS?
SCOTCHGUARD MY BOX
KENT GAMBLE

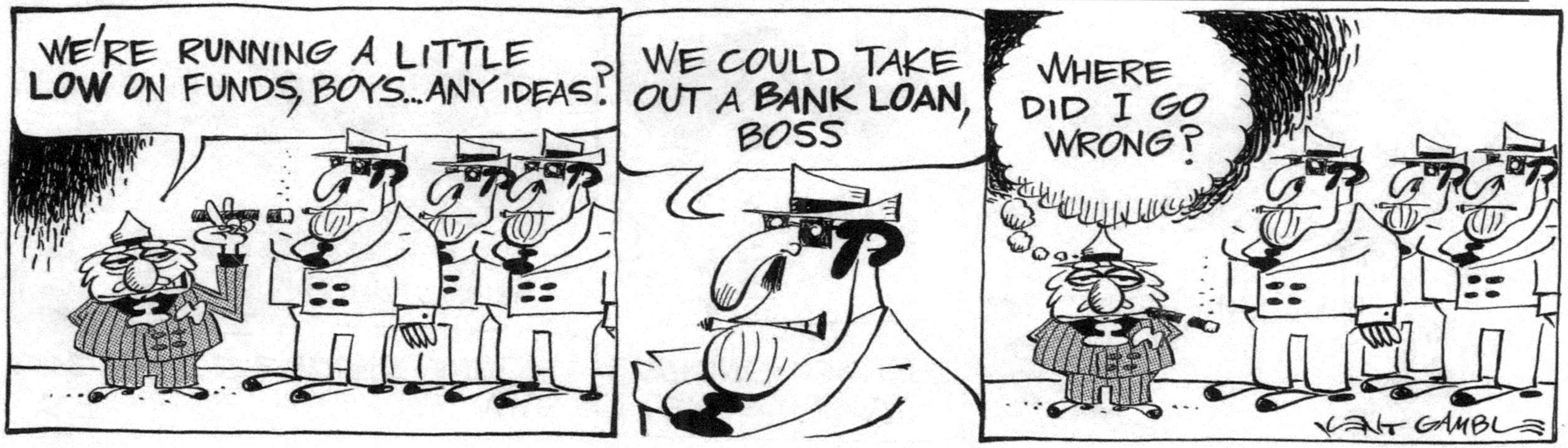
WE'RE RUNNING A LITTLE LOW ON FUNDS, BOYS... ANY IDEAS?
WE COULD TAKE OUT A BANK LOAN, BOSS
WHERE DID I GO WRONG?
KENT GAMBLE

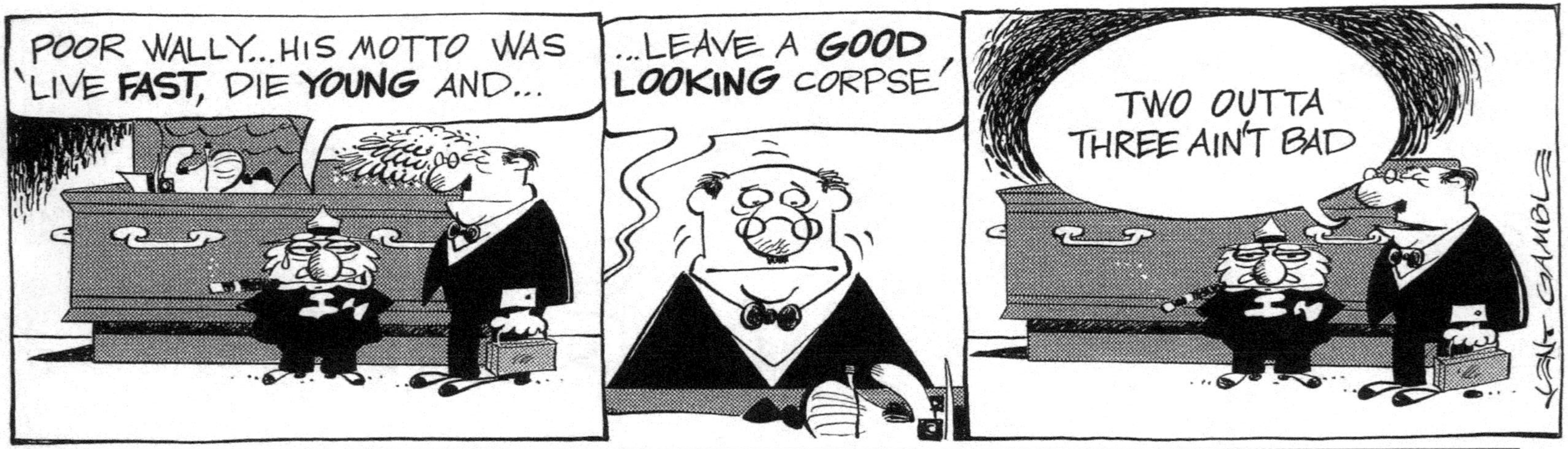
POOR WALLY...HIS MOTTO WAS 'LIVE **FAST**, DIE **YOUNG** AND...
...LEAVE A **GOOD LOOKING** CORPSE'
TWO OUTTA THREE AIN'T BAD
KENT GAMBLE

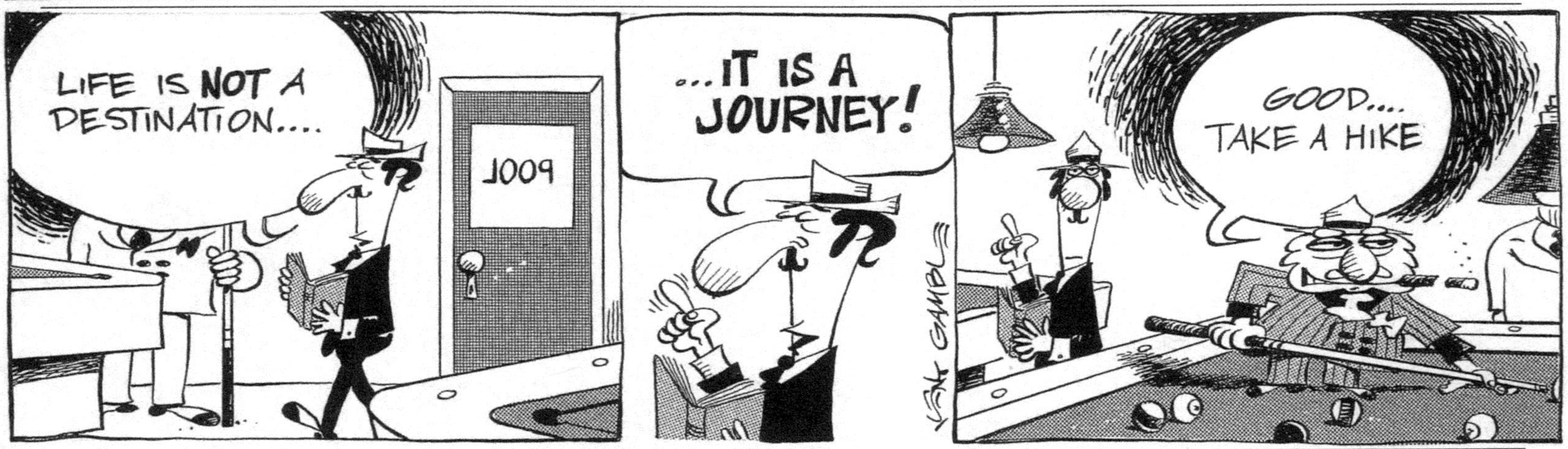
LIFE IS **NOT** A DESTINATION....
POOL
...**IT IS A JOURNEY!**
KENT GAMBLE
GOOD.... TAKE A HIKE

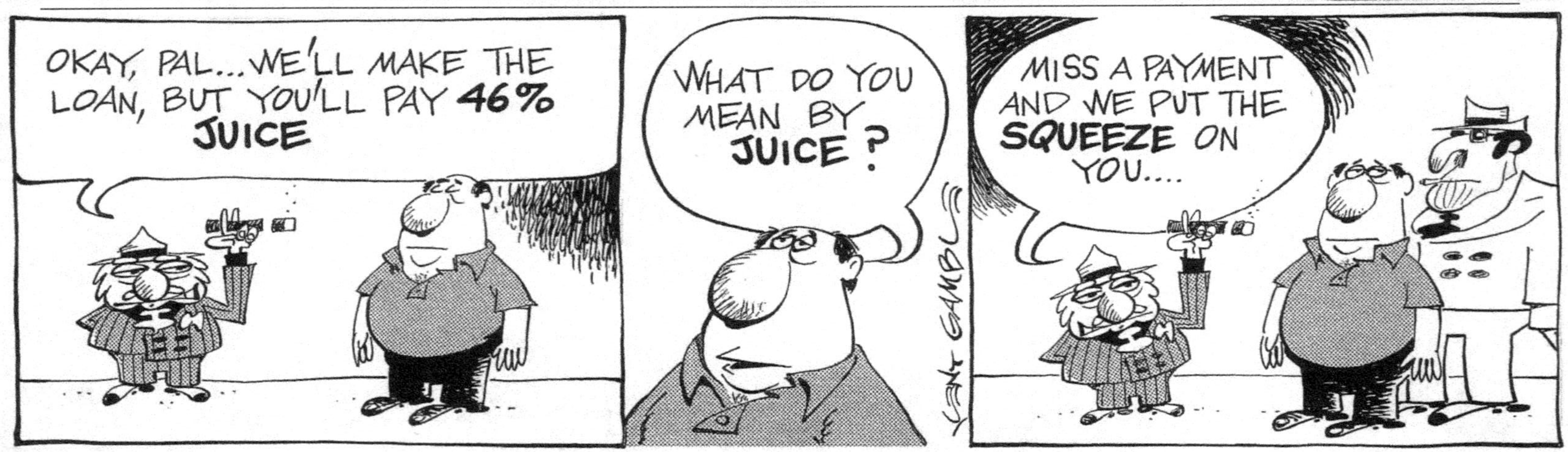
OKAY, PAL...WE'LL MAKE THE LOAN, BUT YOU'LL PAY **46%** **JUICE**
WHAT DO YOU MEAN BY **JUICE**?
KENT GAMBLE
MISS A PAYMENT AND WE PUT THE **SQUEEZE** ON YOU....

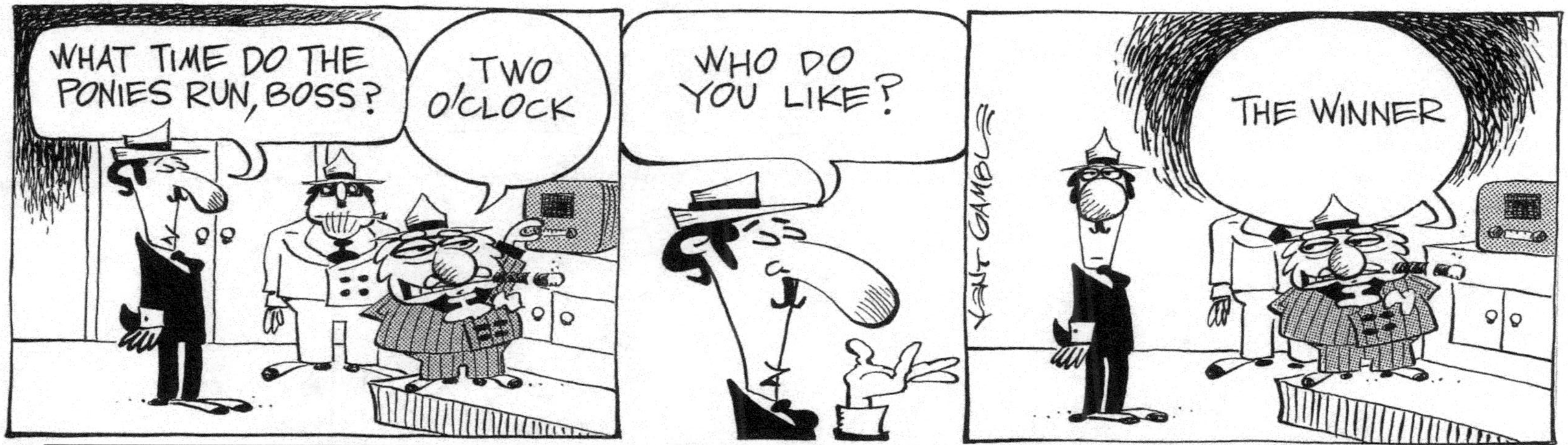
WHAT TIME DO THE PONIES RUN, BOSS?
TWO O'CLOCK
WHO DO YOU LIKE?
THE WINNER
KENT GAMBLE

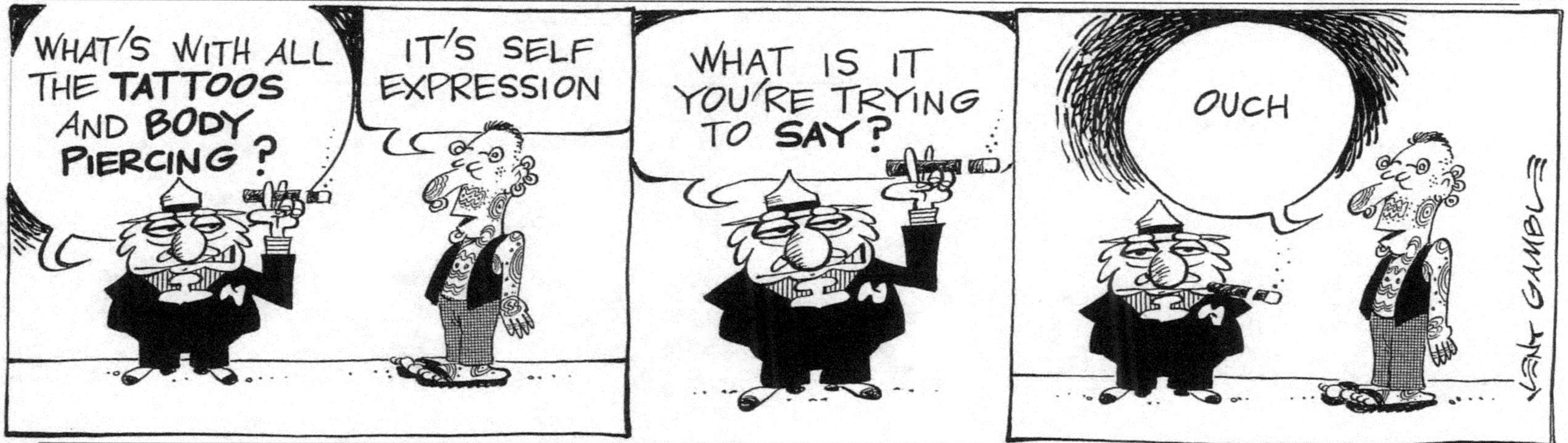
WHAT'S WITH ALL THE **TATTOOS** AND **BODY PIERCING**?
IT'S SELF EXPRESSION
WHAT IS IT YOU'RE TRYING TO **SAY**?
OUCH
KENT GAMBLE

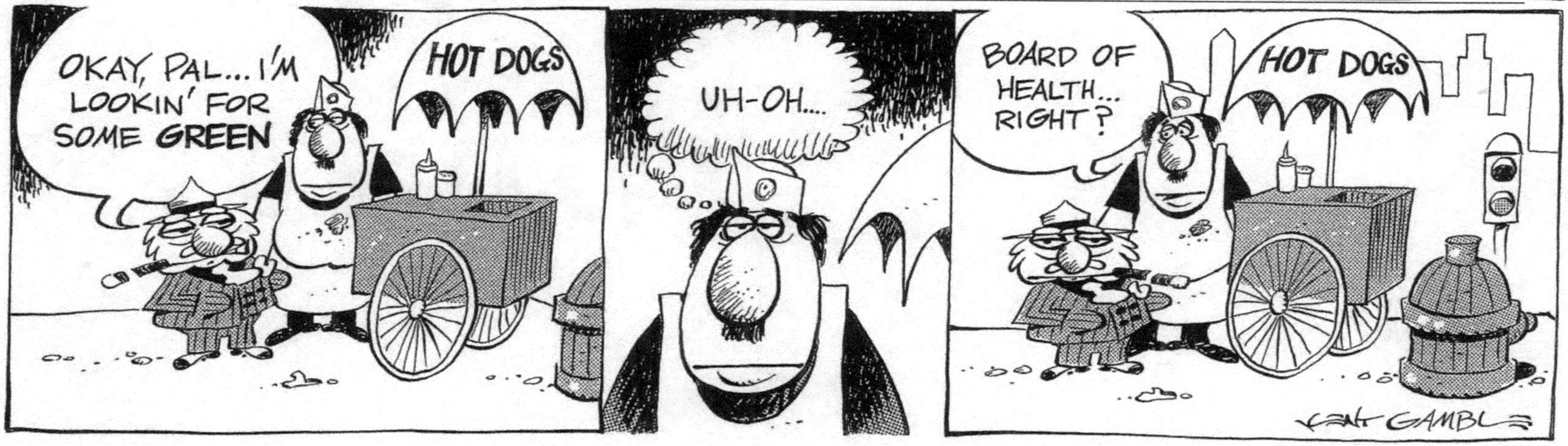
OKAY, PAL... I'M LOOKIN' FOR SOME **GREEN**
HOT DOGS
UH-OH...
BOARD OF HEALTH... RIGHT?
HOT DOGS
KENT GAMBLE

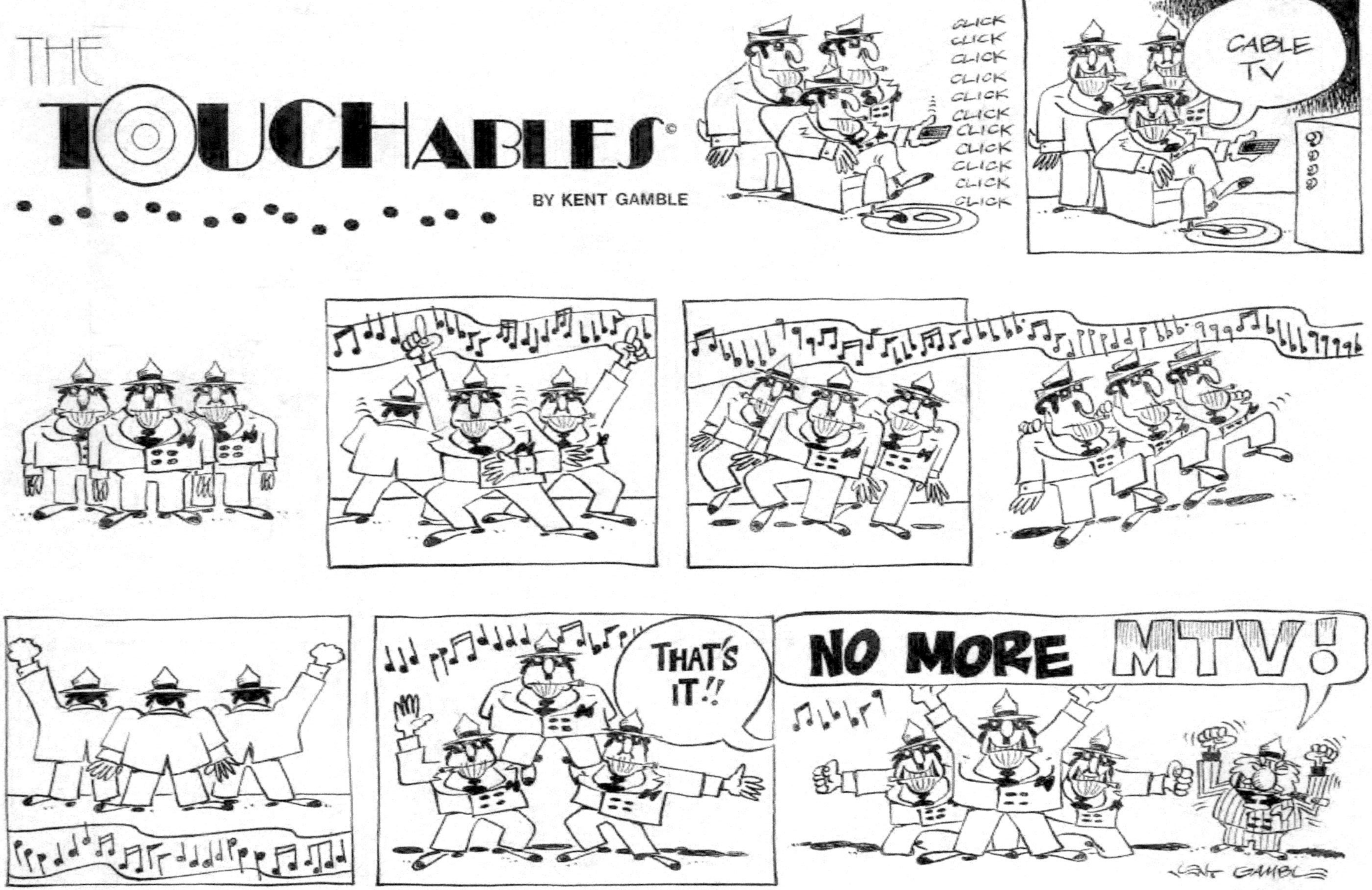
THE TOUCHABLES©
BY KENT GAMBLE
CLICK CLICK CLICK CLICK CLICK CLICK CLICK CLICK CLICK CLICK CLICK
CABLE TV
THAT'S IT!!
NO MORE MTV!
KENT GAMBLE

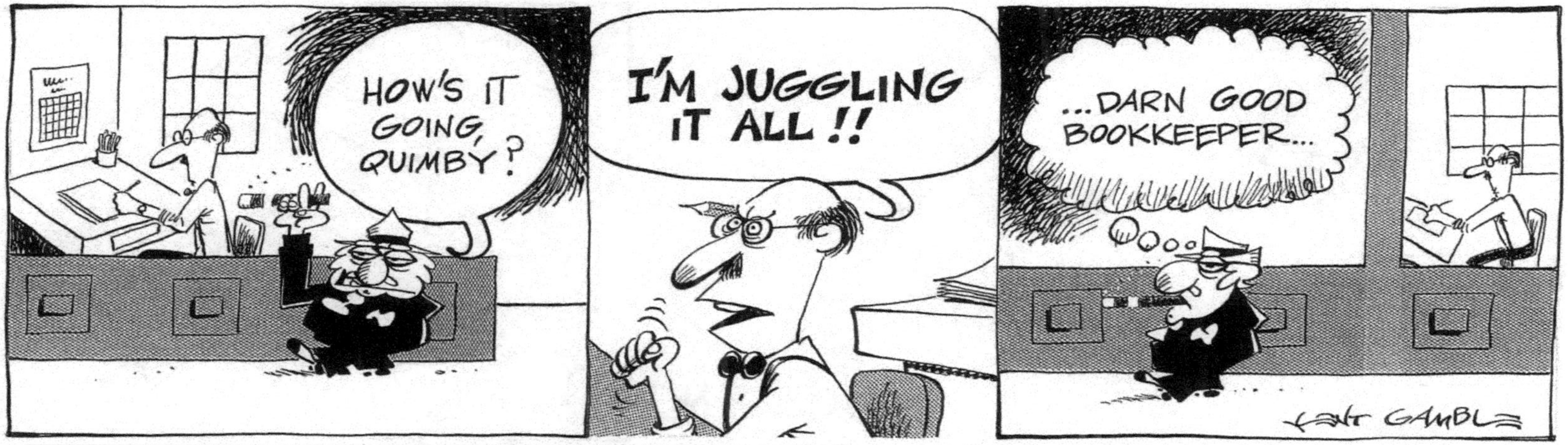
HOW'S IT GOING, QUIMBY?
I'M JUGGLING IT ALL !!
...DARN GOOD BOOKKEEPER...

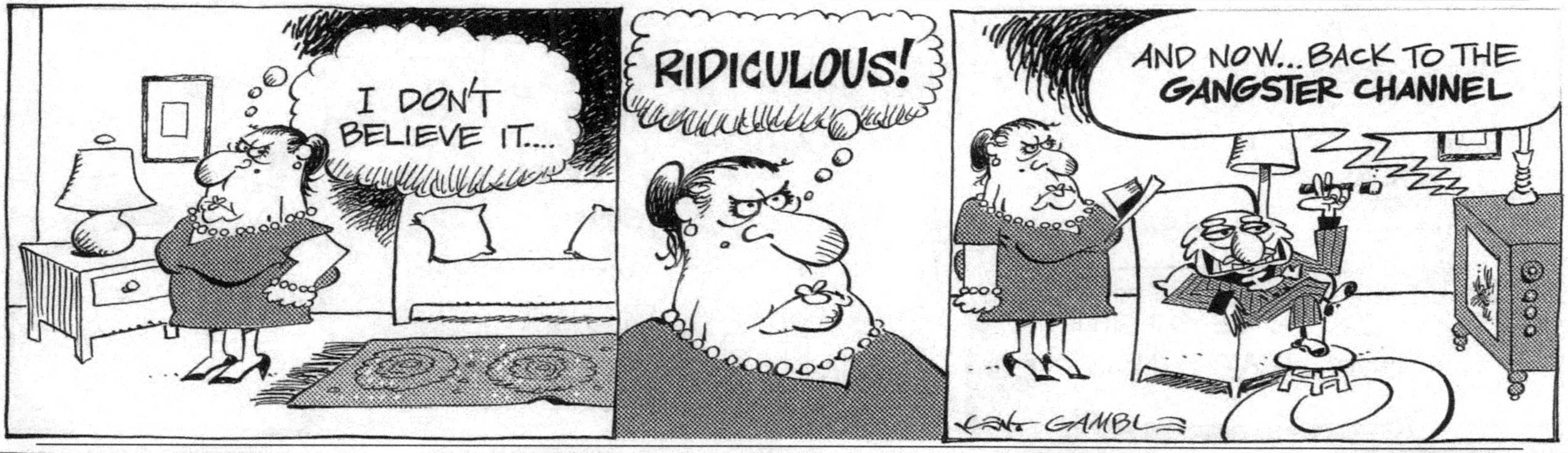
I DON'T BELIEVE IT....
RIDICULOUS!
AND NOW... BACK TO THE GANGSTER CHANNEL

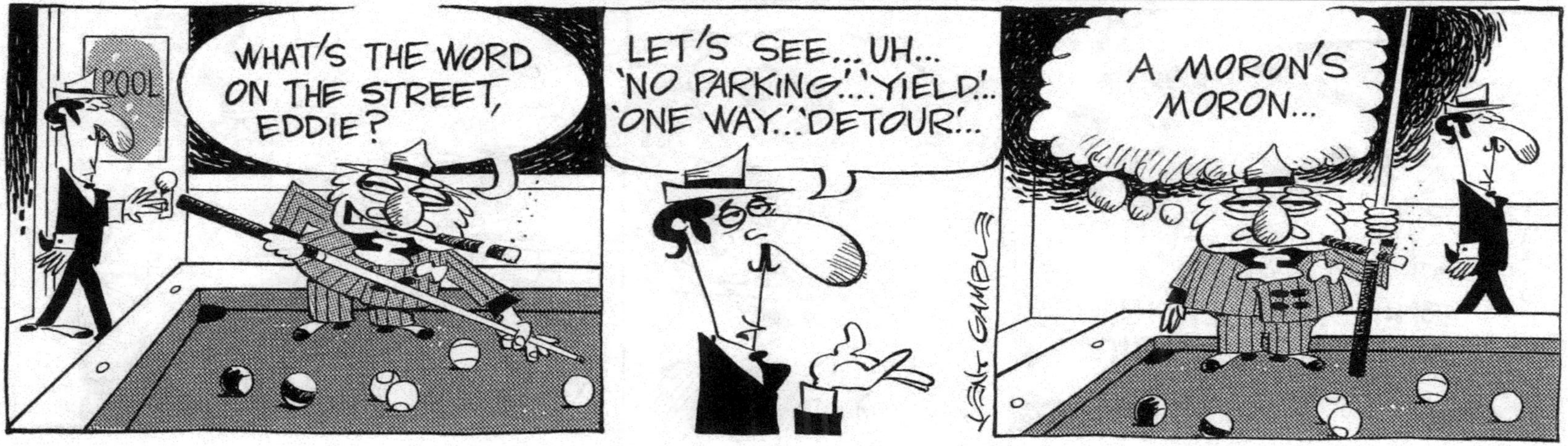
POOL
WHAT'S THE WORD ON THE STREET, EDDIE?
LET'S SEE... UH... 'NO PARKING'... 'YIELD'... 'ONE WAY'... 'DETOUR'...
A MORON'S MORON...

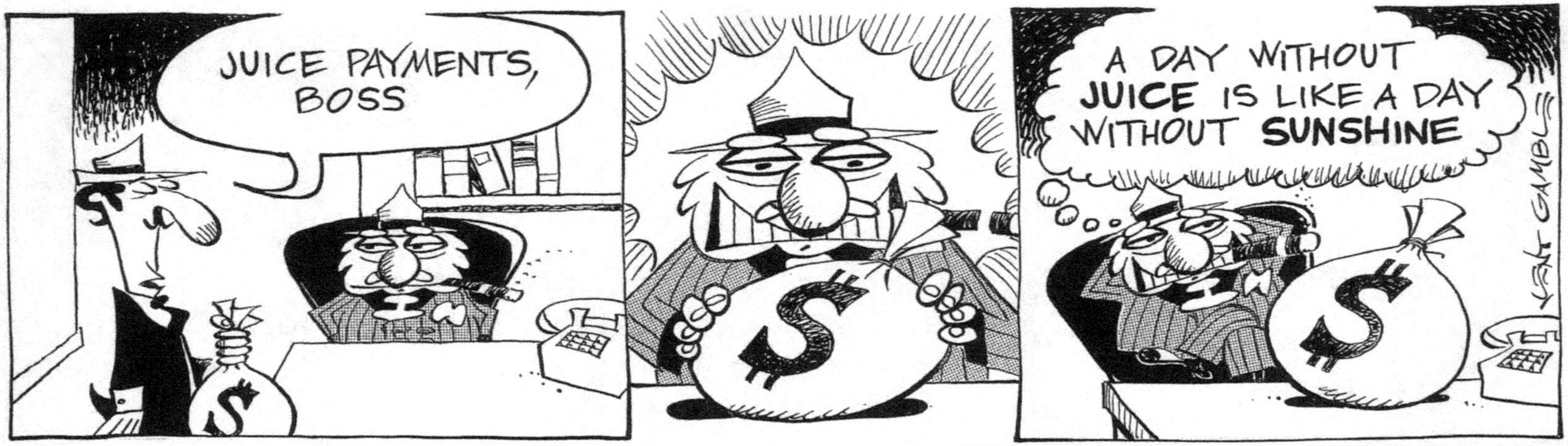
JUICE PAYMENTS, BOSS
A DAY WITHOUT JUICE IS LIKE A DAY WITHOUT SUNSHINE
KENT GAMBLE

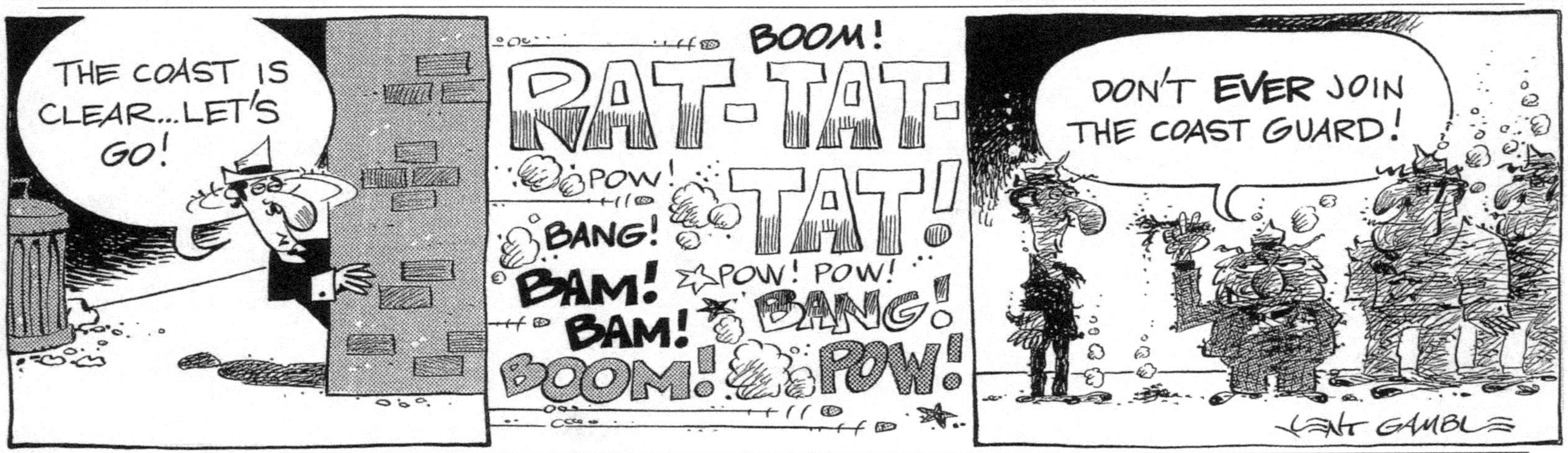
THE COAST IS CLEAR...LET'S GO!
BOOM!
RAT-TAT-TAT!
POW!
BANG!
BAM!
BAM!
POW! POW!
BANG!
BOOM!
POW!
DON'T EVER JOIN THE COAST GUARD!
KENT GAMBLE

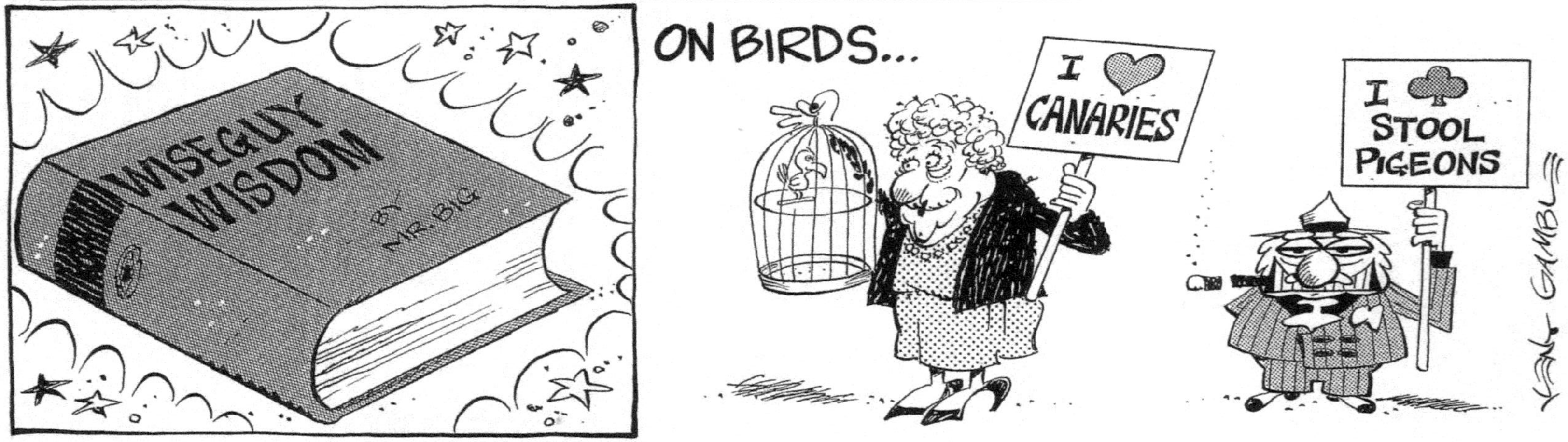
WISEGUY WISDOM
BY MR. BIG
ON BIRDS...
I ♥ CANARIES
I ♣ STOOL PIGEONS
KENT GAMBLE

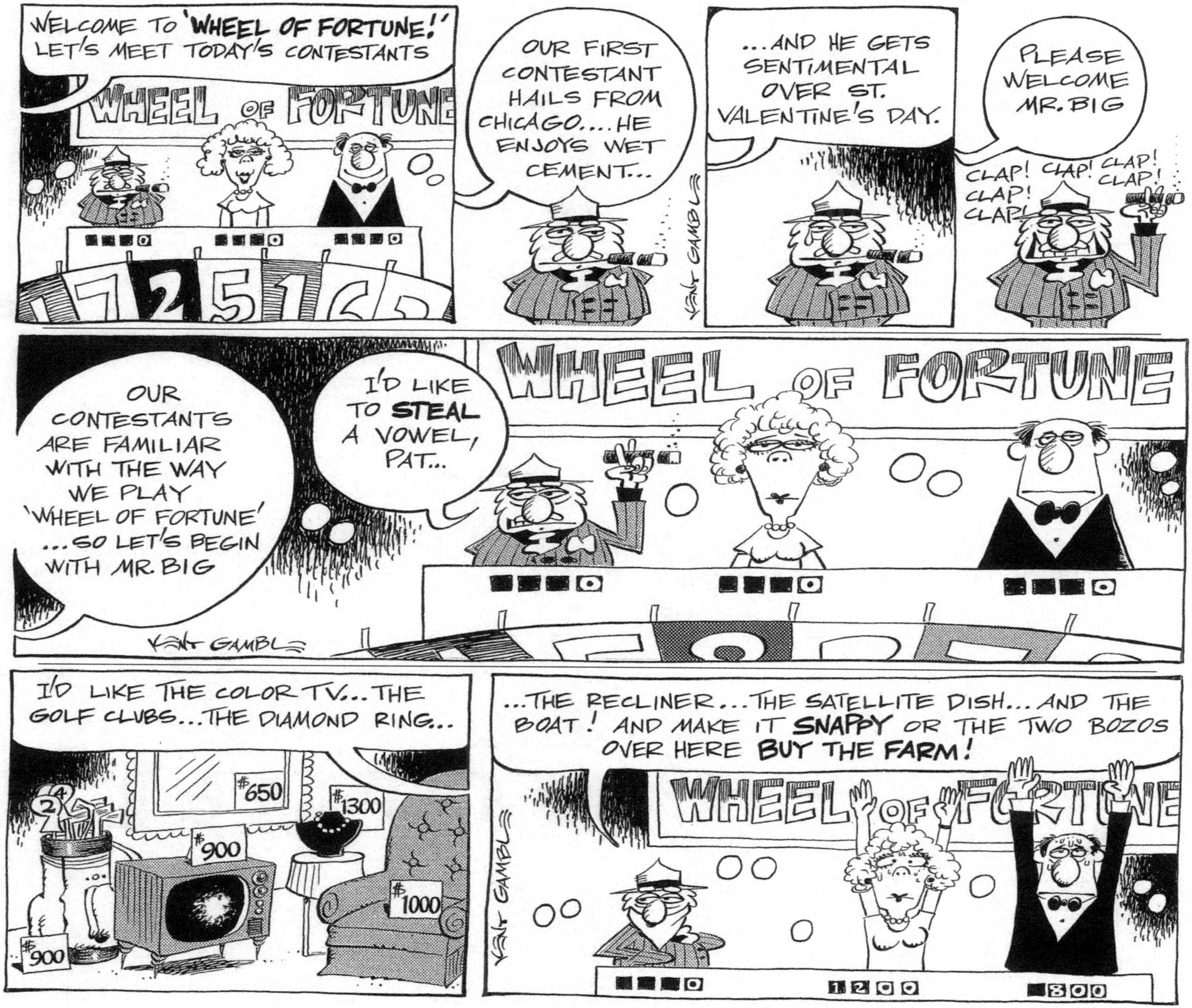
WELCOME TO 'WHEEL OF FORTUNE!' LET'S MEET TODAY'S CONTESTANTS
WHEEL OF FORTUNE
OUR FIRST CONTESTANT HAILS FROM CHICAGO.... HE ENJOYS WET CEMENT...
...AND HE GETS SENTIMENTAL OVER ST. VALENTINE'S DAY.
PLEASE WELCOME MR. BIG
CLAP! CLAP! CLAP! CLAP! CLAP! CLAP!
KENT GAMBLE
WHEEL OF FORTUNE
OUR CONTESTANTS ARE FAMILIAR WITH THE WAY WE PLAY 'WHEEL OF FORTUNE' ...SO LET'S BEGIN WITH MR. BIG
I'D LIKE TO STEAL A VOWEL, PAT...
KENT GAMBLE
I'D LIKE THE COLOR TV... THE GOLF CLUBS... THE DIAMOND RING...
$650
$1300
$900
$1000
$900
...THE RECLINER... THE SATELLITE DISH... AND THE BOAT! AND MAKE IT SNAPPY OR THE TWO BOZOS OVER HERE BUY THE FARM!
WHEEL OF FORTUNE
1200
800
KENT GAMBLE

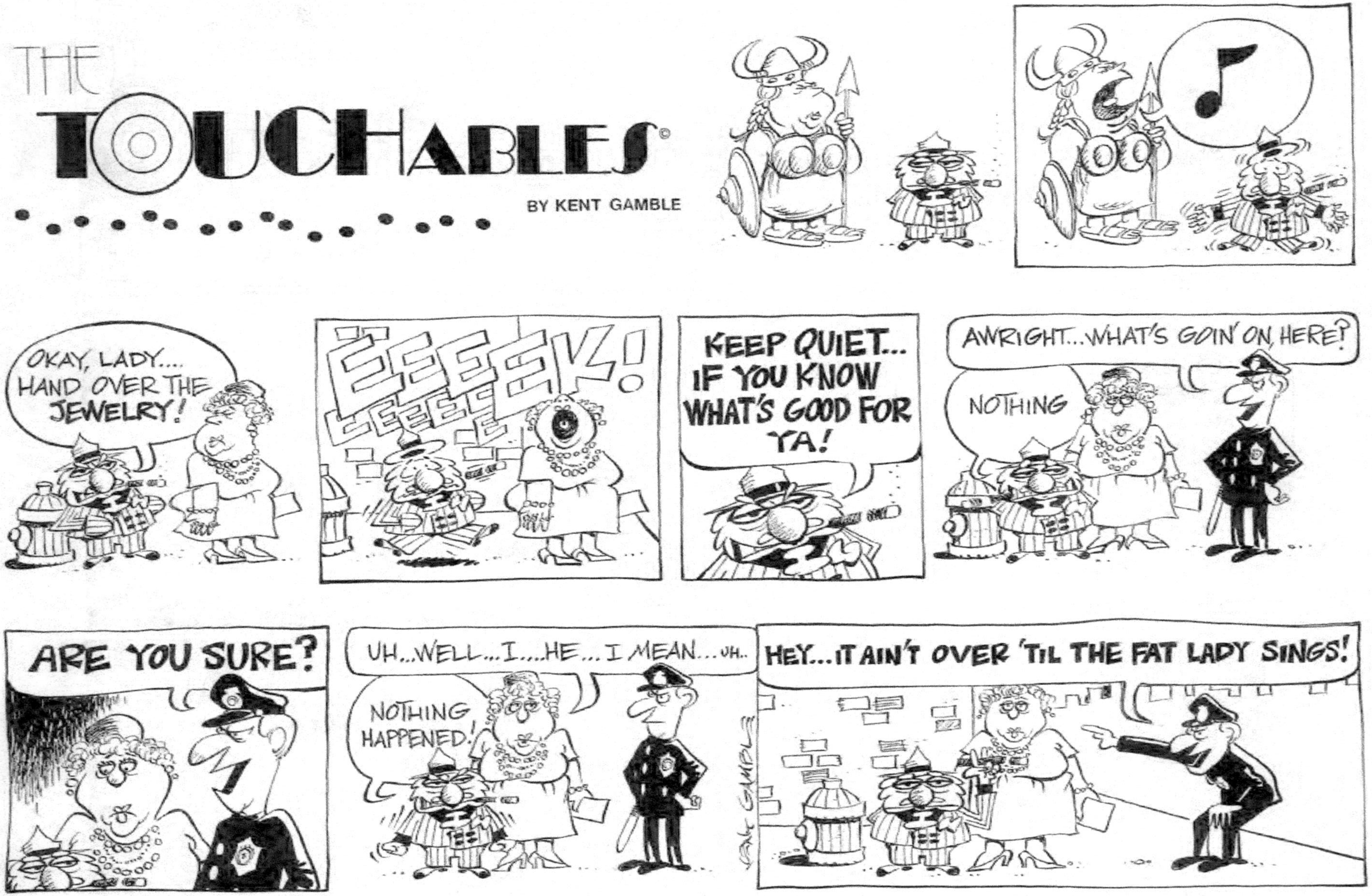
THE TOUCHABLES©
BY KENT GAMBLE
OKAY, LADY.... HAND OVER THE JEWELRY!
EEEEEK!
KEEP QUIET... IF YOU KNOW WHAT'S GOOD FOR YA!
AWRIGHT...WHAT'S GOIN' ON, HERE?
NOTHING
ARE YOU SURE?
UH...WELL...I....HE...I MEAN...UH..
NOTHING HAPPENED!
HEY...IT AIN'T OVER 'TIL THE FAT LADY SINGS!

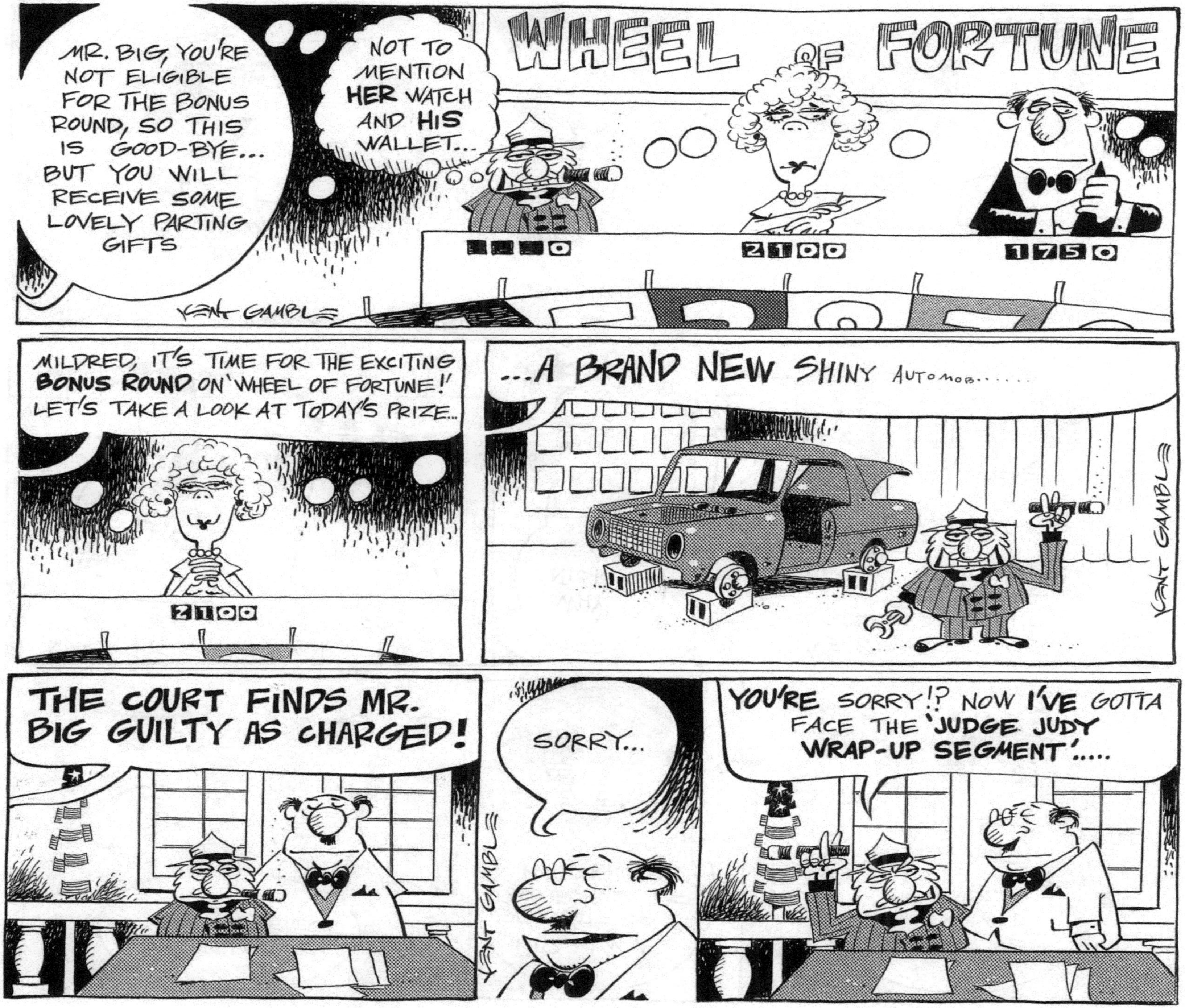
MR. BIG, YOU'RE NOT ELIGIBLE FOR THE BONUS ROUND, SO THIS IS GOOD-BYE... BUT YOU WILL RECEIVE SOME LOVELY PARTING GIFTS
NOT TO MENTION HER WATCH AND HIS WALLET...
WHEEL OF FORTUNE
2100
1750
KENT GAMBLE
MILDRED, IT'S TIME FOR THE EXCITING BONUS ROUND ON 'WHEEL OF FORTUNE!' LET'S TAKE A LOOK AT TODAY'S PRIZE...
2100
...A BRAND NEW SHINY AUTOMOB......
KENT GAMBLE
THE COURT FINDS MR. BIG GUILTY AS CHARGED!
SORRY...
KENT GAMBLE
YOU'RE SORRY!? NOW I'VE GOTTA FACE THE 'JUDGE JUDY WRAP-UP SEGMENT'.....

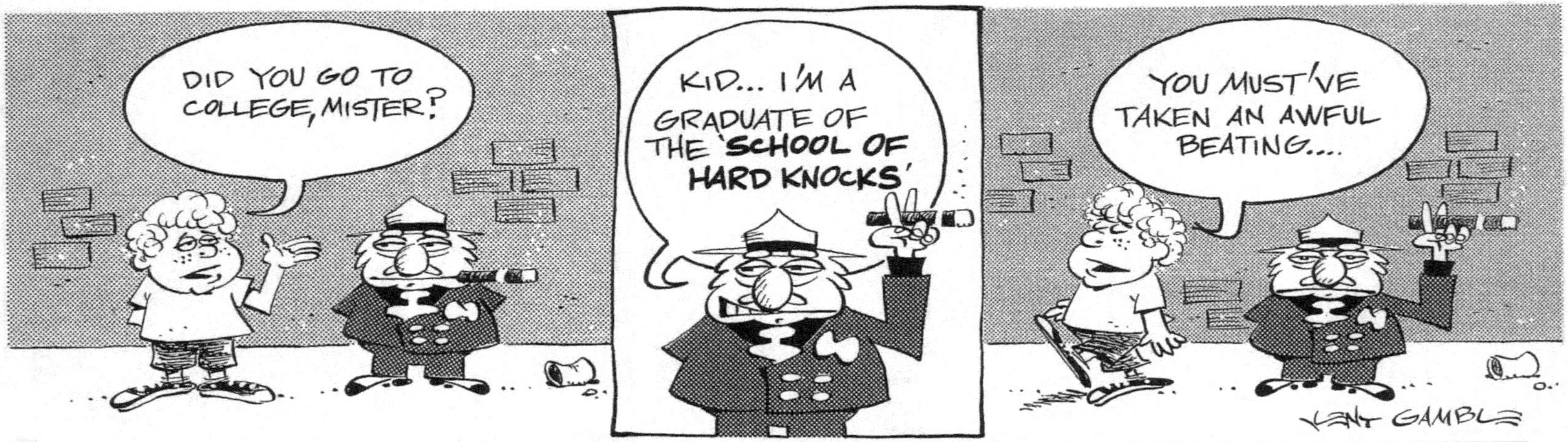
DID YOU GO TO COLLEGE, MISTER?
KID... I'M A GRADUATE OF THE 'SCHOOL OF HARD KNOCKS'
YOU MUST'VE TAKEN AN AWFUL BEATING....
KENT GAMBLE

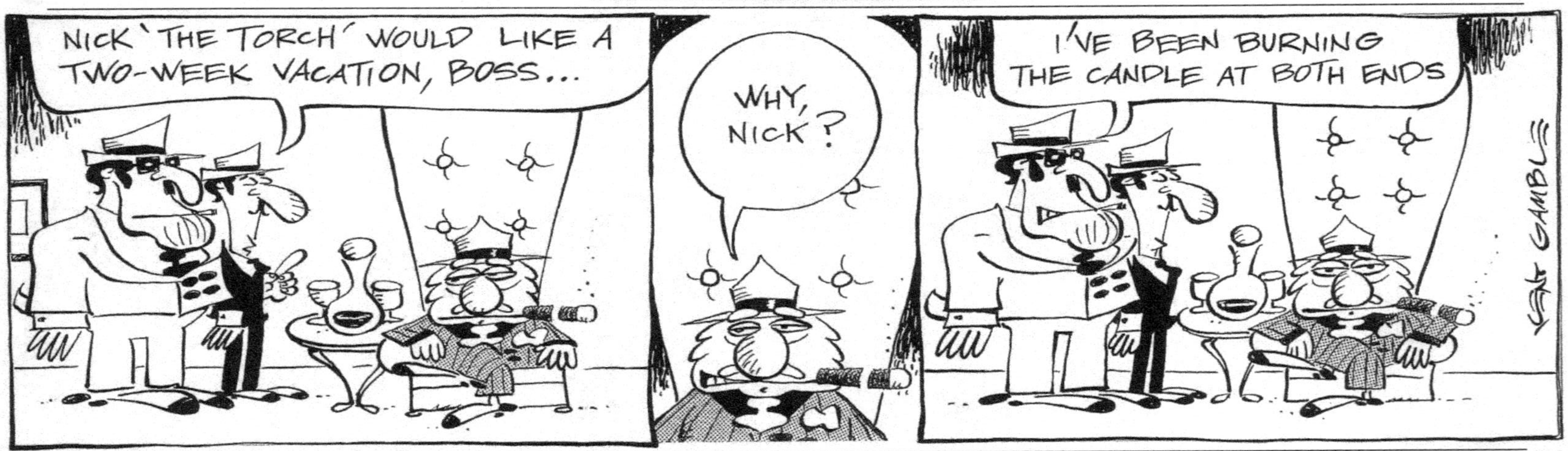
NICK 'THE TORCH' WOULD LIKE A TWO-WEEK VACATION, BOSS...
WHY, NICK?
I'VE BEEN BURNING THE CANDLE AT BOTH ENDS
KENT GAMBLE

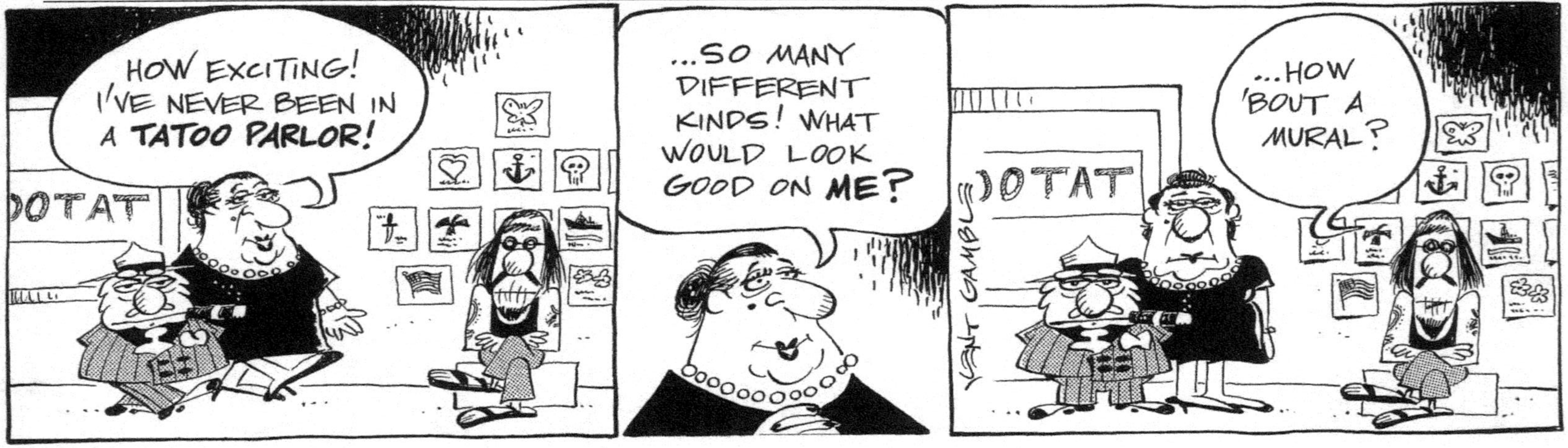
HOW EXCITING! I'VE NEVER BEEN IN A TATOO PARLOR!
TATOO
...SO MANY DIFFERENT KINDS! WHAT WOULD LOOK GOOD ON ME?
...HOW 'BOUT A MURAL?
TATOO
KENT GAMBLE

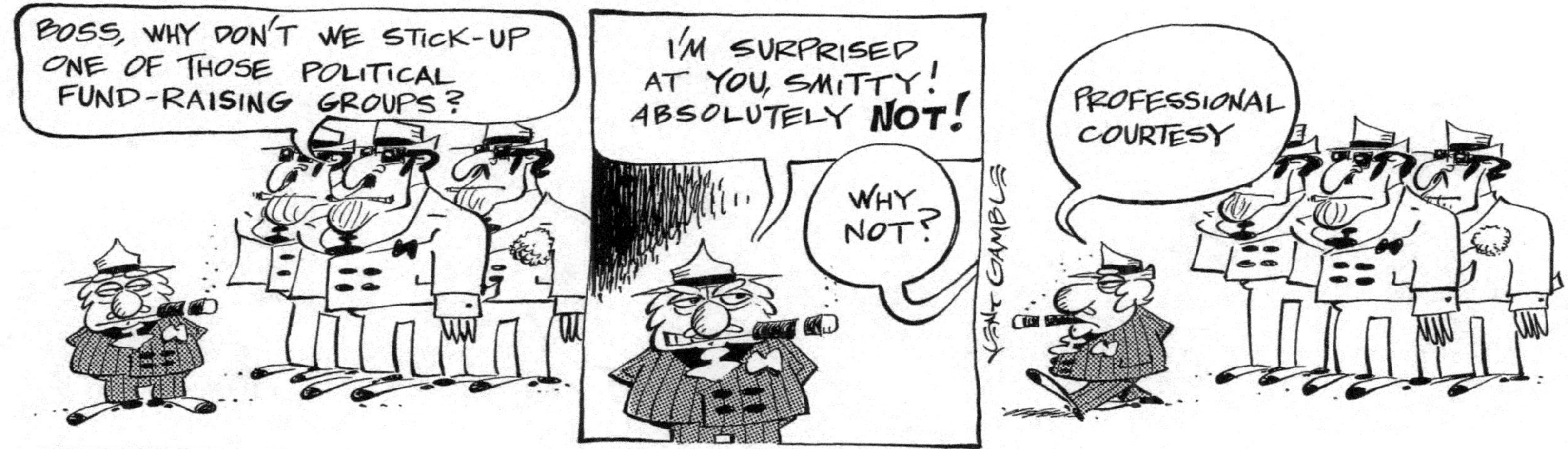
BOSS, WHY DON'T WE STICK-UP ONE OF THOSE POLITICAL FUND-RAISING GROUPS?
I'M SURPRISED AT YOU, SMITTY! ABSOLUTELY NOT!
WHY NOT?
PROFESSIONAL COURTESY
KENT GAMBLE

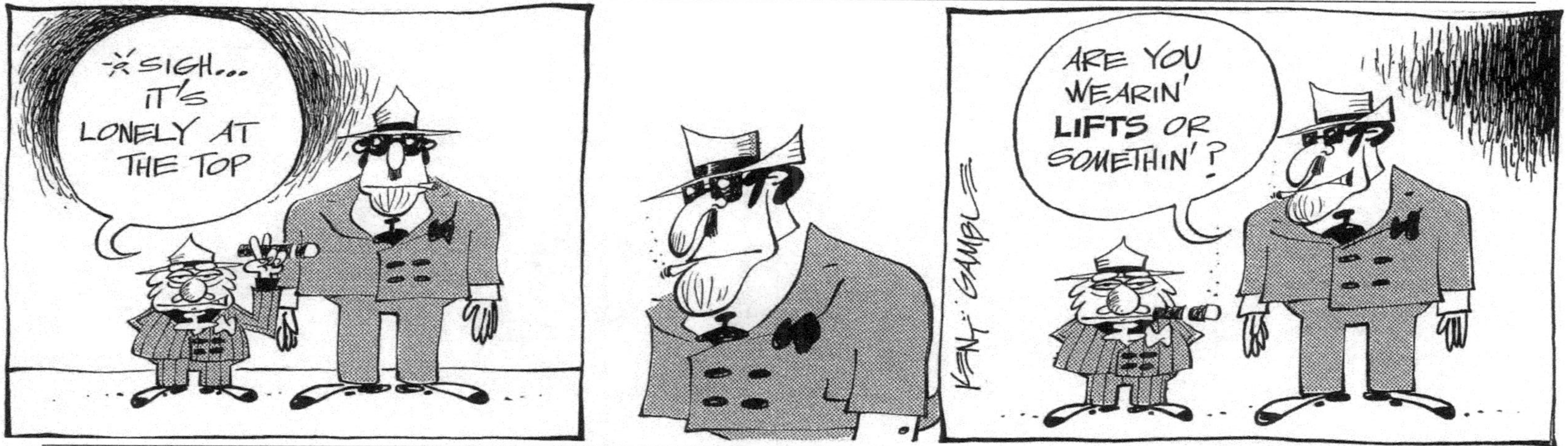
*SIGH... IT'S LONELY AT THE TOP
ARE YOU WEARIN' LIFTS OR SOMETHIN'?
KENT GAMBLE

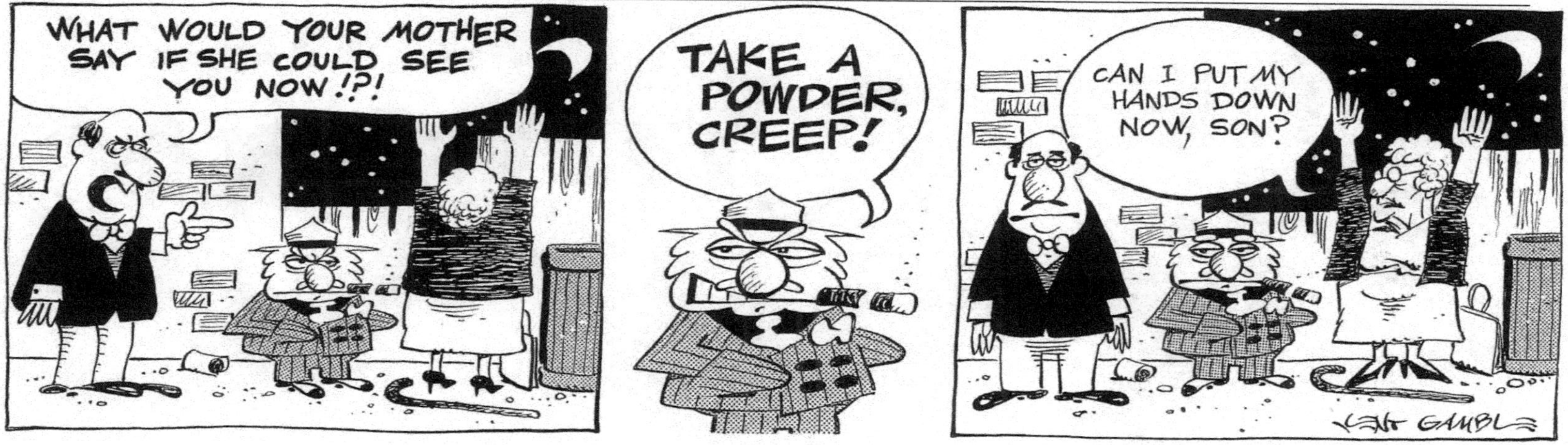
WHAT WOULD YOUR MOTHER SAY IF SHE COULD SEE YOU NOW!?!
TAKE A POWDER, CREEP!
CAN I PUT MY HANDS DOWN NOW, SON?
KENT GAMBLE

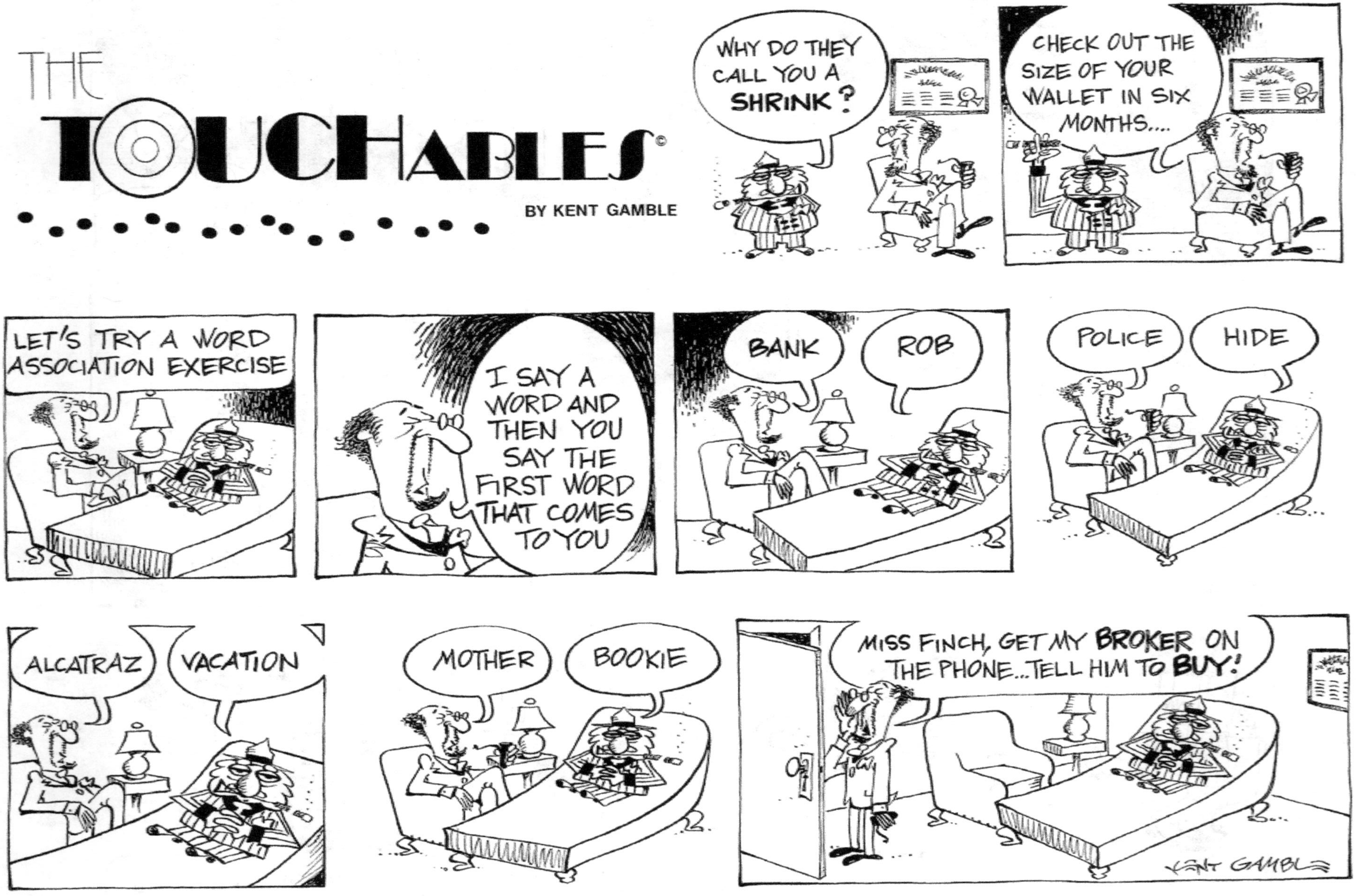
THE TOUCHABLES©
BY KENT GAMBLE
WHY DO THEY CALL YOU A SHRINK?
CHECK OUT THE SIZE OF YOUR WALLET IN SIX MONTHS....
LET'S TRY A WORD ASSOCIATION EXERCISE
I SAY A WORD AND THEN YOU SAY THE FIRST WORD THAT COMES TO YOU
BANK
ROB
POLICE
HIDE
ALCATRAZ
VACATION
MOTHER
BOOKIE
MISS FINCH, GET MY BROKER ON THE PHONE...TELL HIM TO BUY!
KENT GAMBLE

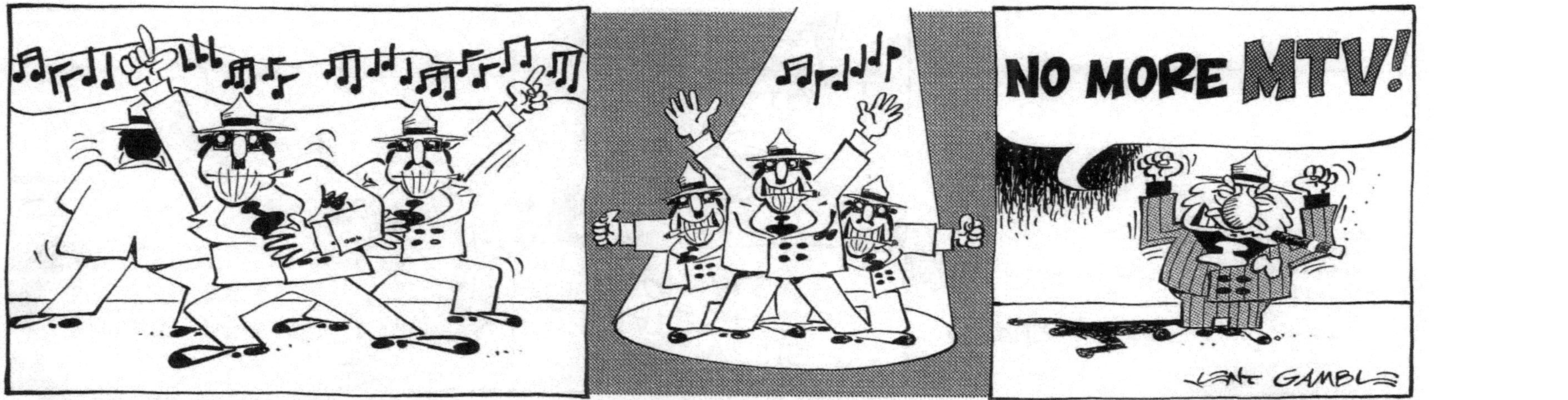
NO MORE MTV!
KENT GAMBLE

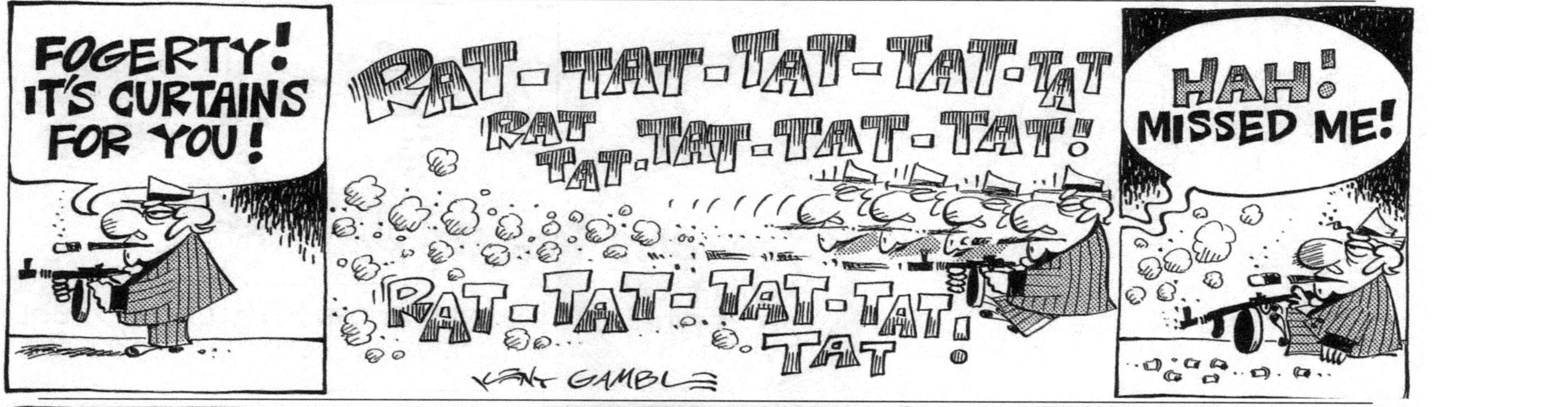
FOGERTY! IT'S CURTAINS FOR YOU!
RAT-TAT-TAT-TAT-TAT
RAT TAT-TAT-TAT-TAT!
RAT-TAT-TAT-TAT-TAT! TAT
HAH! MISSED ME!
KENT GAMBLE

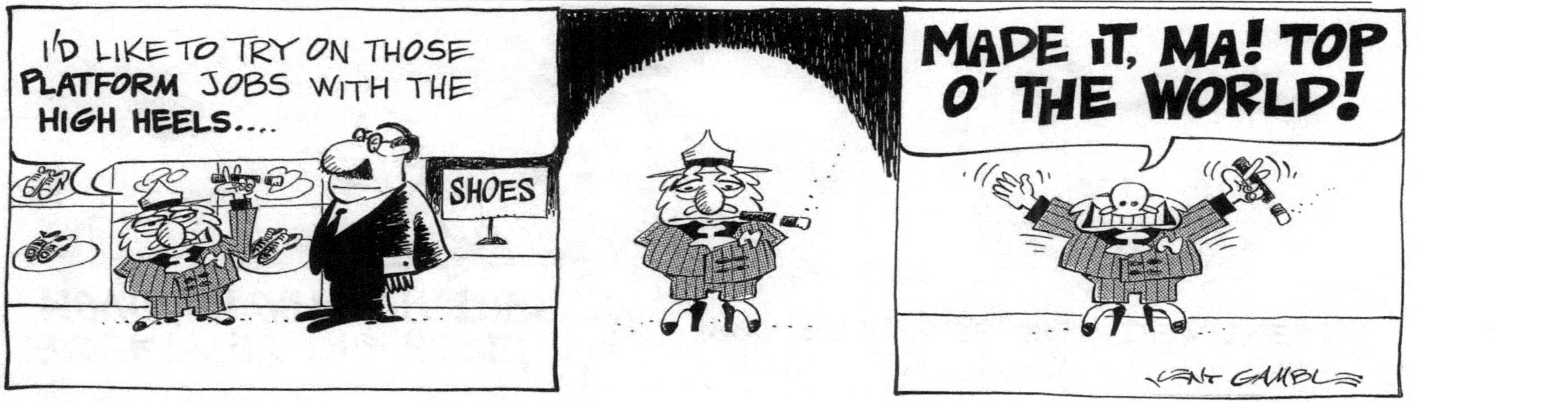
I'D LIKE TO TRY ON THOSE PLATFORM JOBS WITH THE HIGH HEELS....
SHOES
MADE IT, MA! TOP O' THE WORLD!
KENT GAMBLE

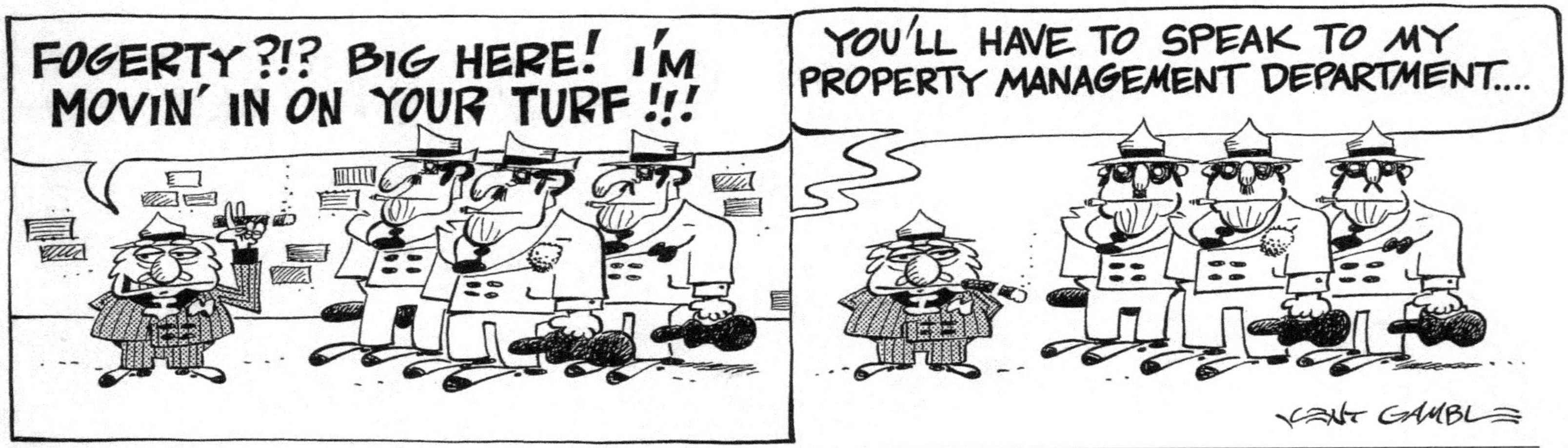
FOGERTY ?!? BIG HERE! I'M MOVIN' IN ON YOUR TURF !!!
YOU'LL HAVE TO SPEAK TO MY PROPERTY MANAGEMENT DEPARTMENT....
KENT GAMBLE

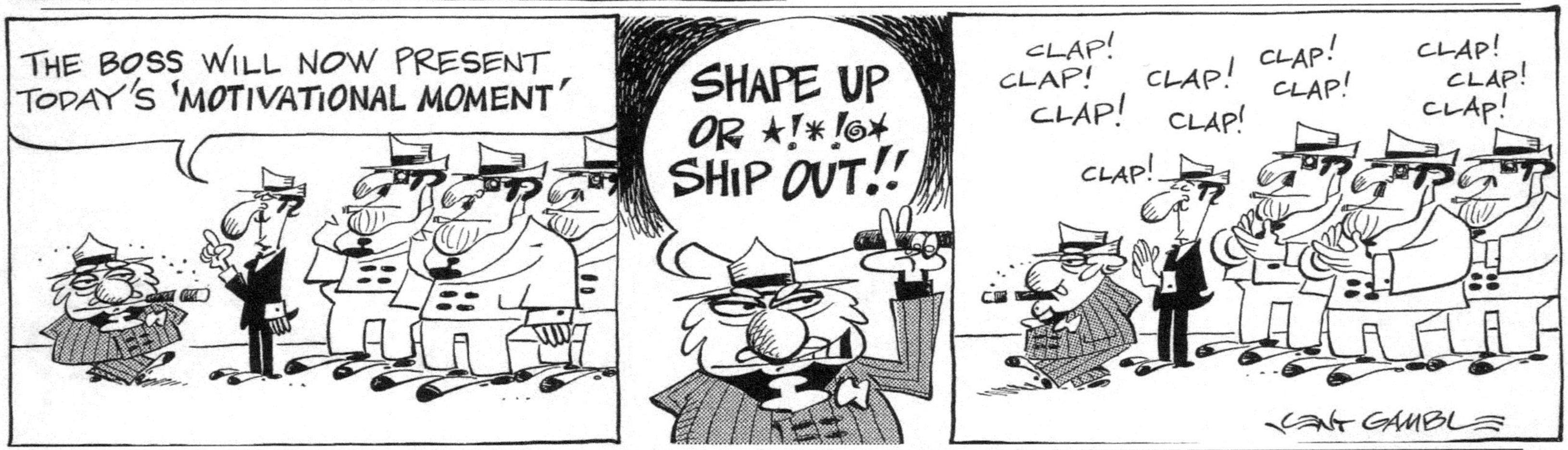
THE BOSS WILL NOW PRESENT TODAY'S 'MOTIVATIONAL MOMENT'
SHAPE UP OR *!*!@* SHIP OUT!!
CLAP! CLAP! CLAP! CLAP! CLAP! CLAP! CLAP! CLAP! CLAP! CLAP! CLAP!
KENT GAMBLE

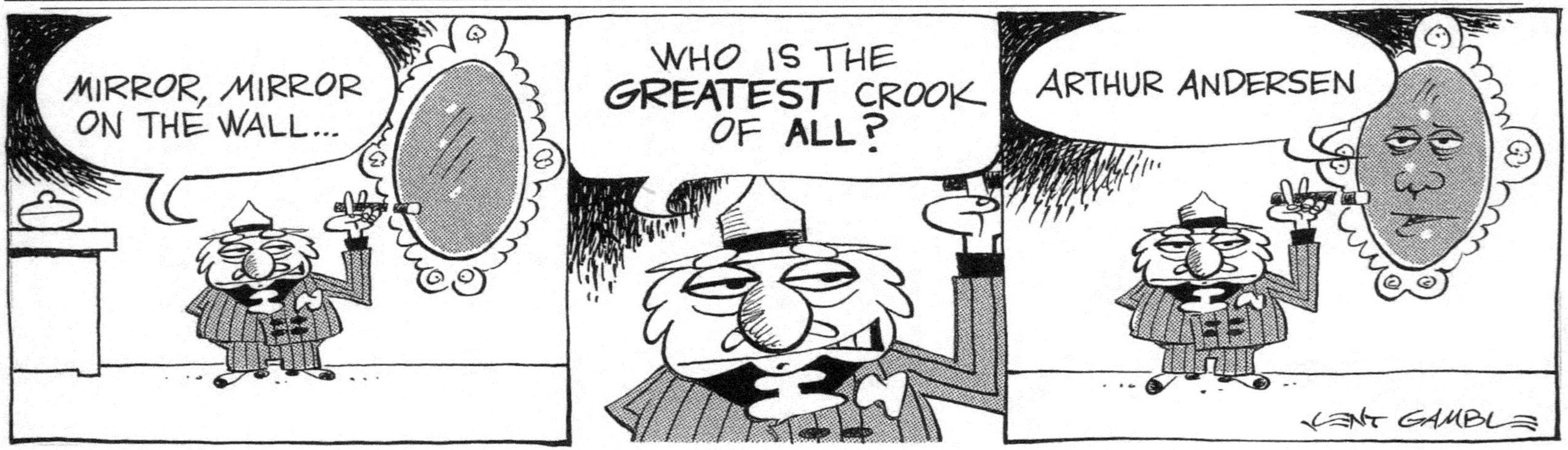
MIRROR, MIRROR ON THE WALL...
WHO IS THE GREATEST CROOK OF ALL?
ARTHUR ANDERSEN
KENT GAMBLE

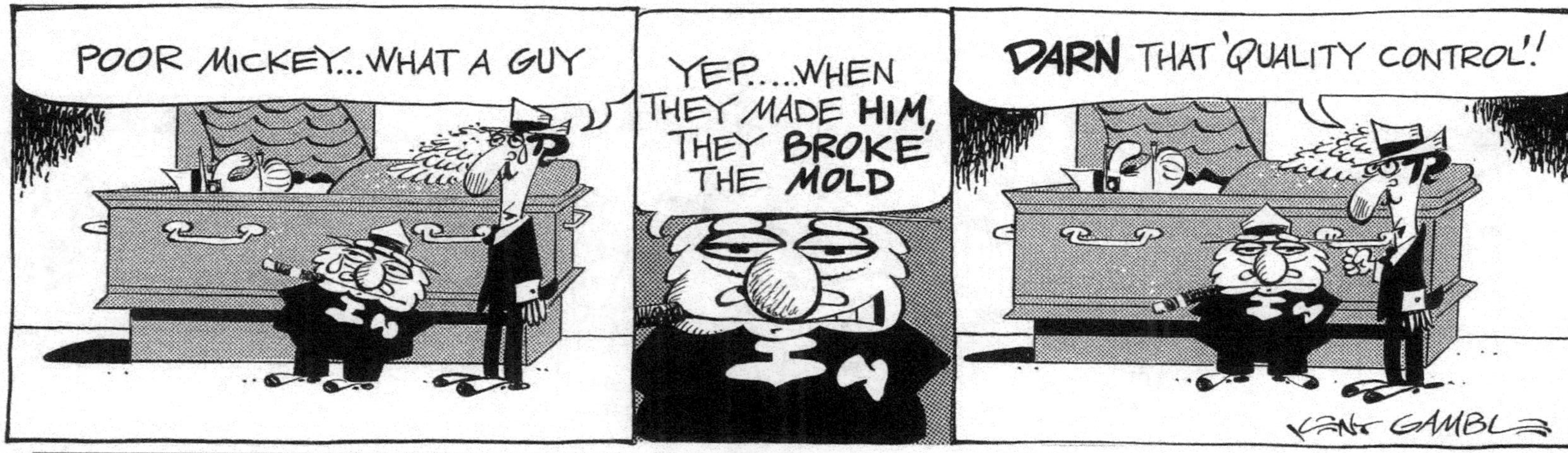
POOR MICKEY...WHAT A GUY
YEP.....WHEN THEY MADE **HIM**, THEY **BROKE** THE **MOLD**
DARN THAT 'QUALITY CONTROL'!
KENT GAMBLE

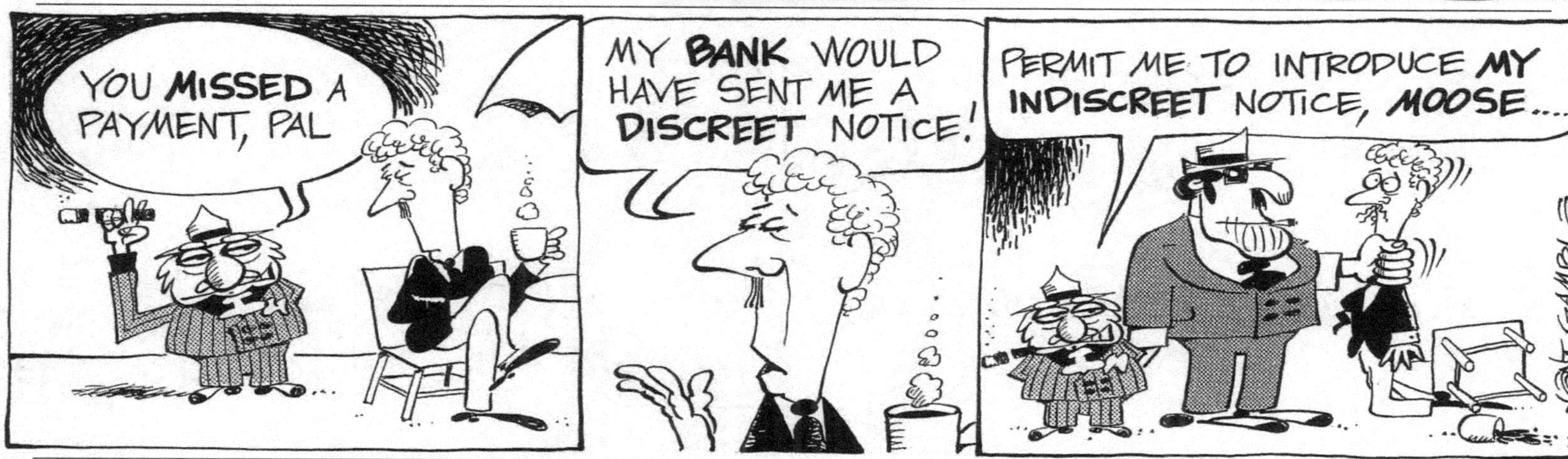
YOU **MISSED** A PAYMENT, PAL
MY **BANK** WOULD HAVE SENT ME A **DISCREET** NOTICE!
PERMIT ME TO INTRODUCE **MY INDISCREET** NOTICE, **MOOSE**....
KENT GAMBLE

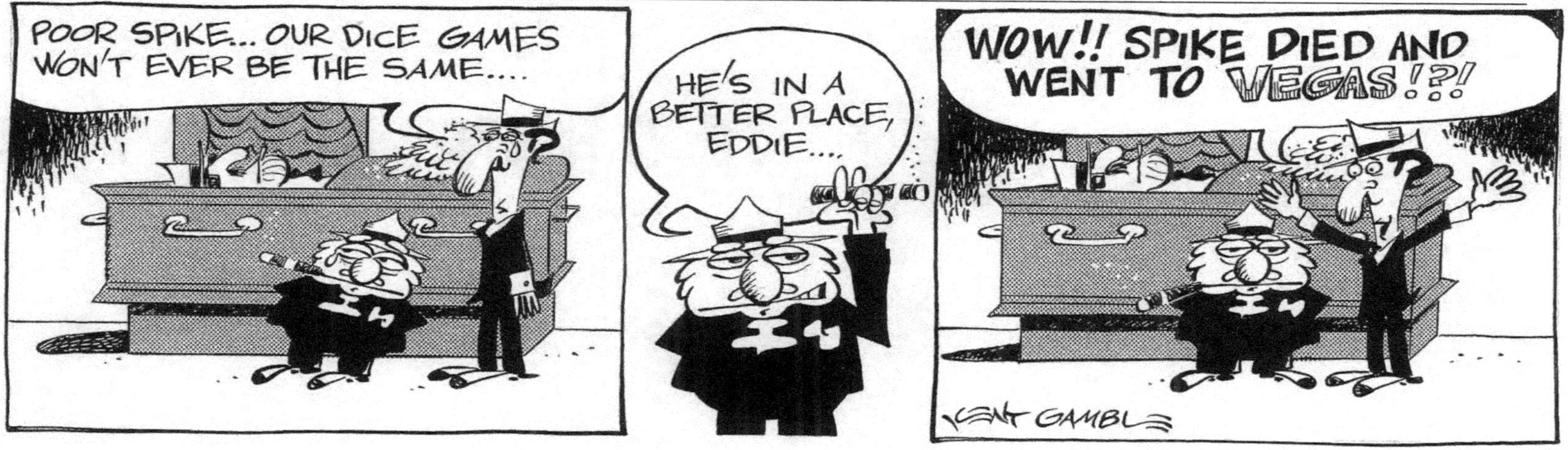
POOR SPIKE... OUR DICE GAMES WON'T EVER BE THE SAME....
HE'S IN A BETTER PLACE, EDDIE....
WOW!! SPIKE DIED AND WENT TO VEGAS!?!
KENT GAMBLE

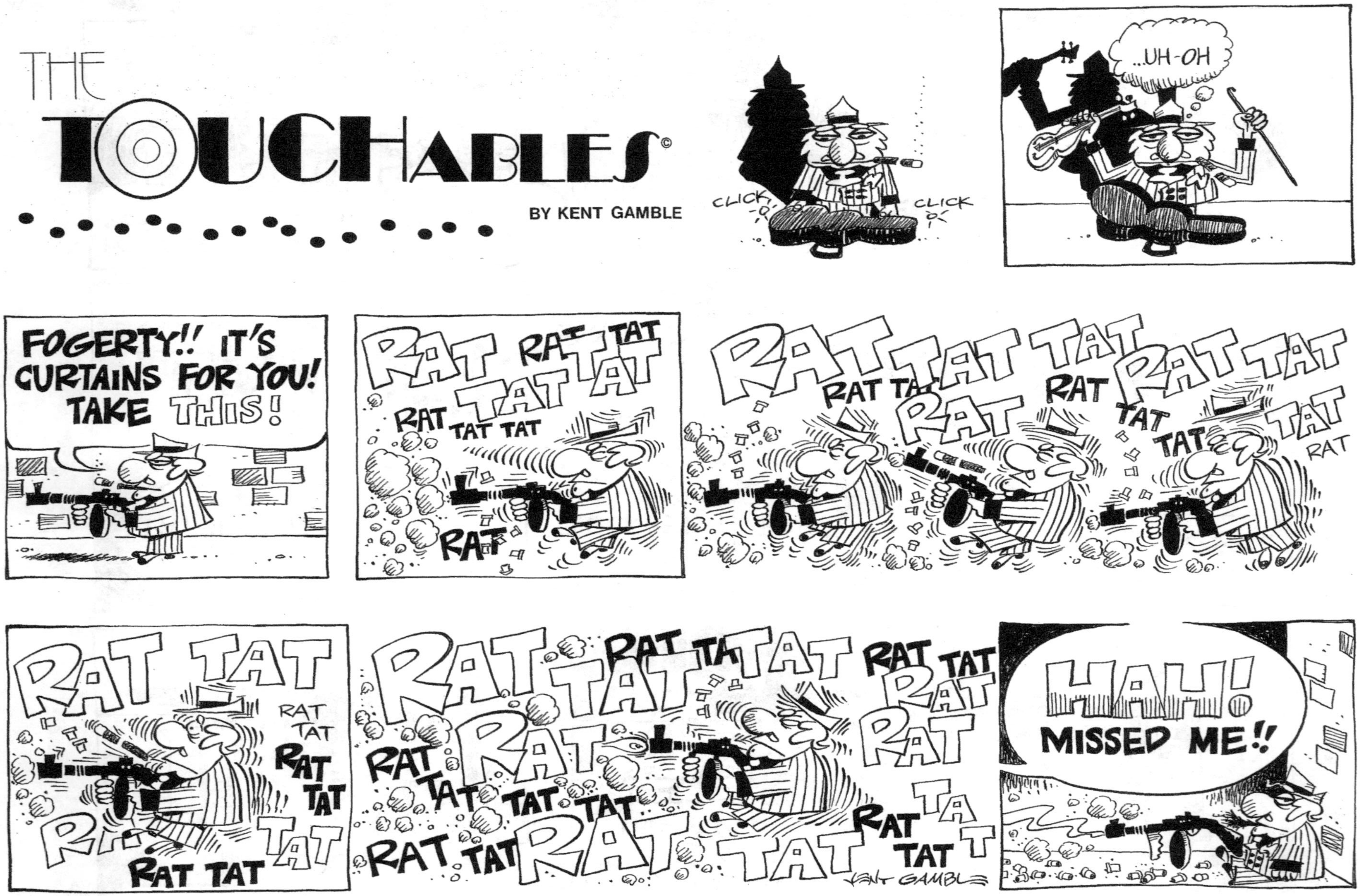
THE TOUCHABLES©
BY KENT GAMBLE
CLICK
CLICK
..UH-OH
FOGERTY!! IT'S CURTAINS FOR YOU! TAKE THIS!
RAT RAT TAT TAT TAT
RAT TAT TAT
RAT
RAT TAT TAT TAT RAT TAT RAT RAT RAT TAT TAT TAT TAT RAT
RAT TAT RAT TAT RAT TAT TAT RAT TAT
RAT TAT RAT TAT RAT TAT RAT TAT RAT RAT
RAT TAT TAT TAT RAT TAT RAT RAT TAT TA TAT T
KENT GAMBLE
HAH! MISSED ME!!

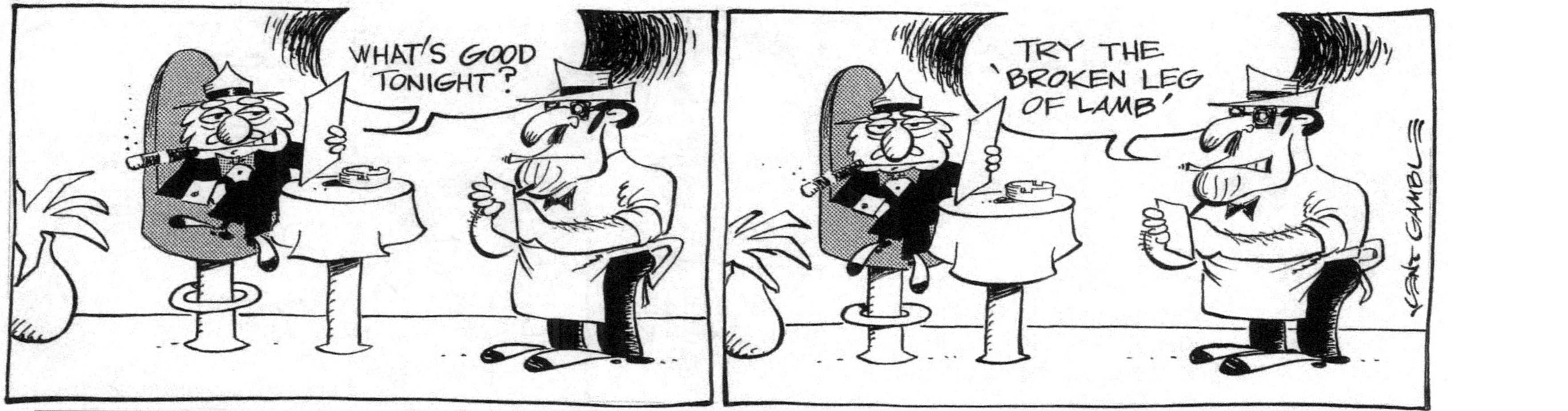
WHAT'S GOOD TONIGHT?
TRY THE 'BROKEN LEG OF LAMB'
KENT GAMBLE

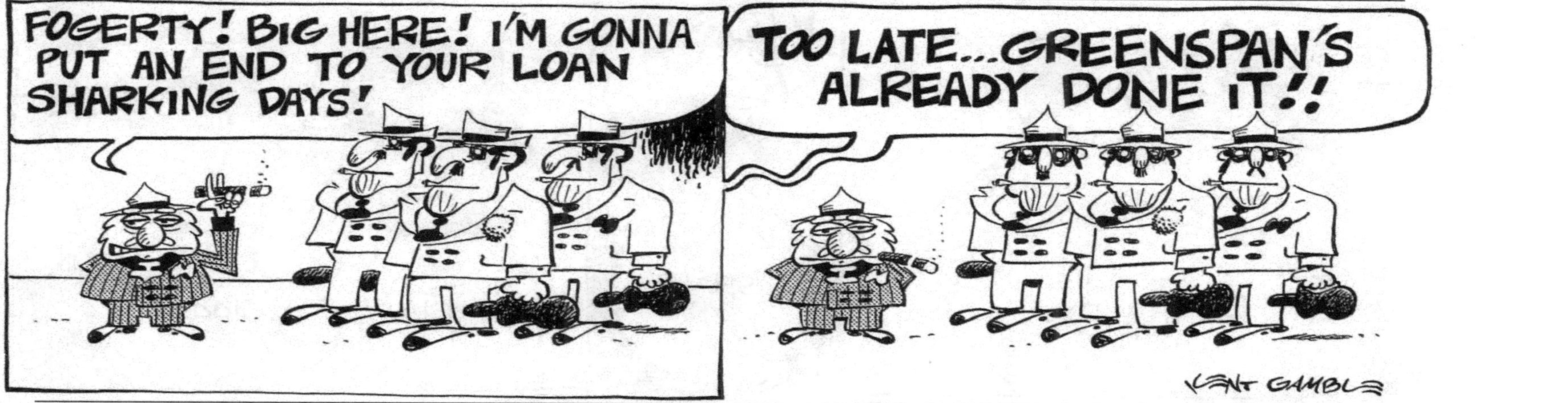
FOGERTY! BIG HERE! I'M GONNA PUT AN END TO YOUR LOAN SHARKING DAYS!
TOO LATE...GREENSPAN'S ALREADY DONE IT!!
KENT GAMBLE

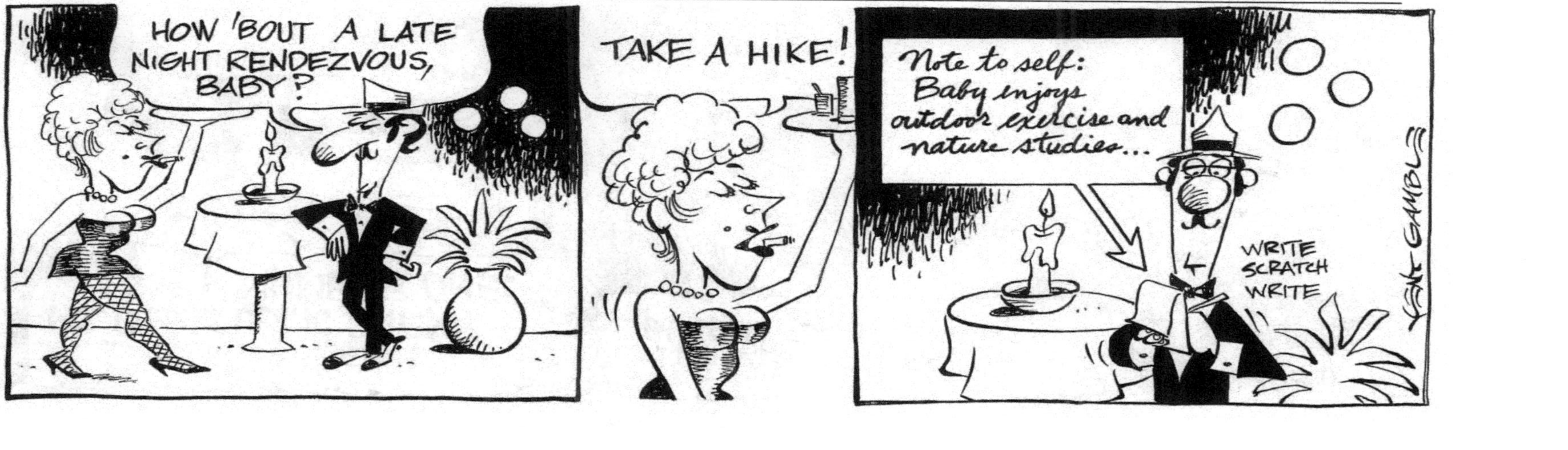
HOW 'BOUT A LATE NIGHT RENDEZVOUS, BABY?
TAKE A HIKE!
Note to self: Baby enjoys outdoor exercise and nature studies...
WRITE SCRATCH WRITE
KENT GAMBLE

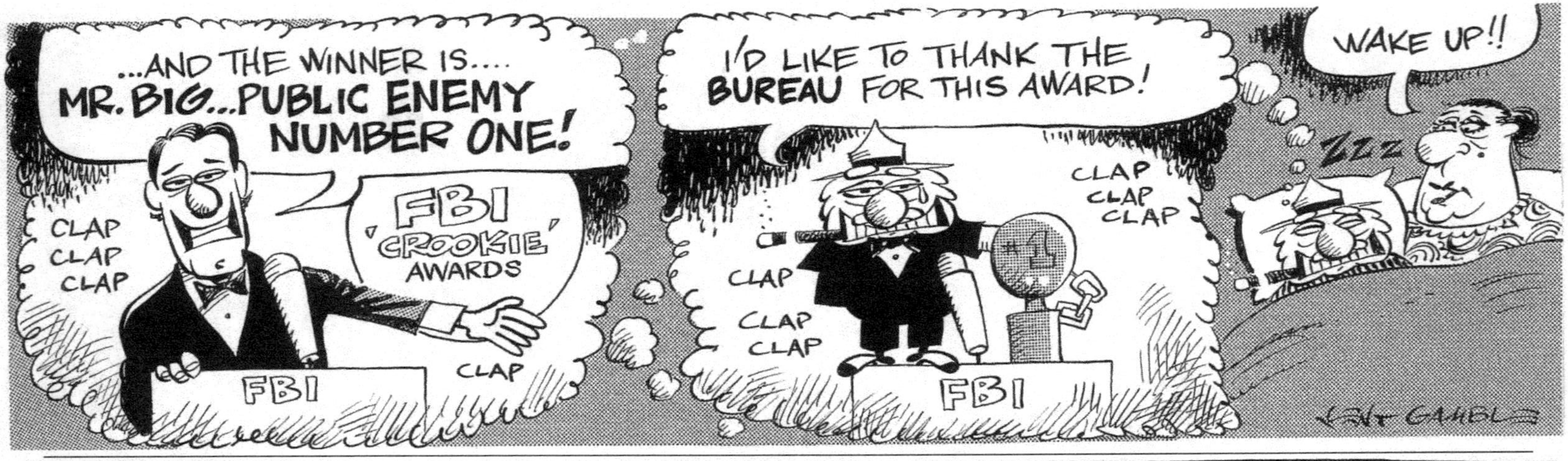
...AND THE WINNER IS.... MR. BIG...PUBLIC ENEMY NUMBER ONE!
FBI 'CROOKIE' AWARDS
CLAP CLAP CLAP
CLAP
FBI
I'D LIKE TO THANK THE BUREAU FOR THIS AWARD!
CLAP
CLAP CLAP
CLAP CLAP CLAP
FBI
WAKE UP!!
ZZZ
KENT GAMBLE

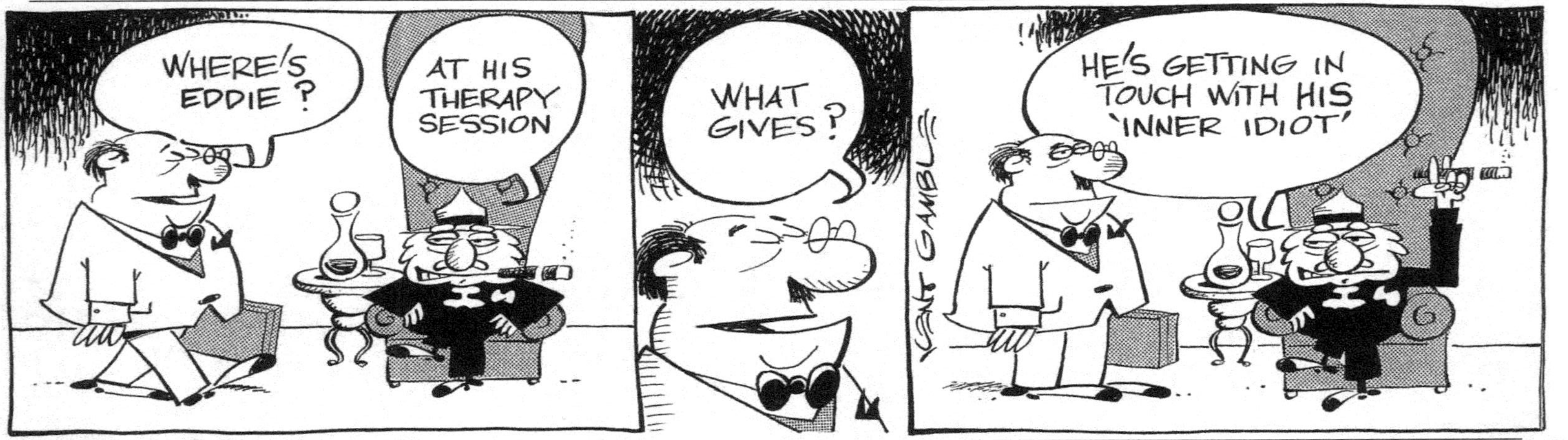
WHERE'S EDDIE ?
AT HIS THERAPY SESSION
WHAT GIVES ?
HE'S GETTING IN TOUCH WITH HIS 'INNER IDIOT'
KENT GAMBLE

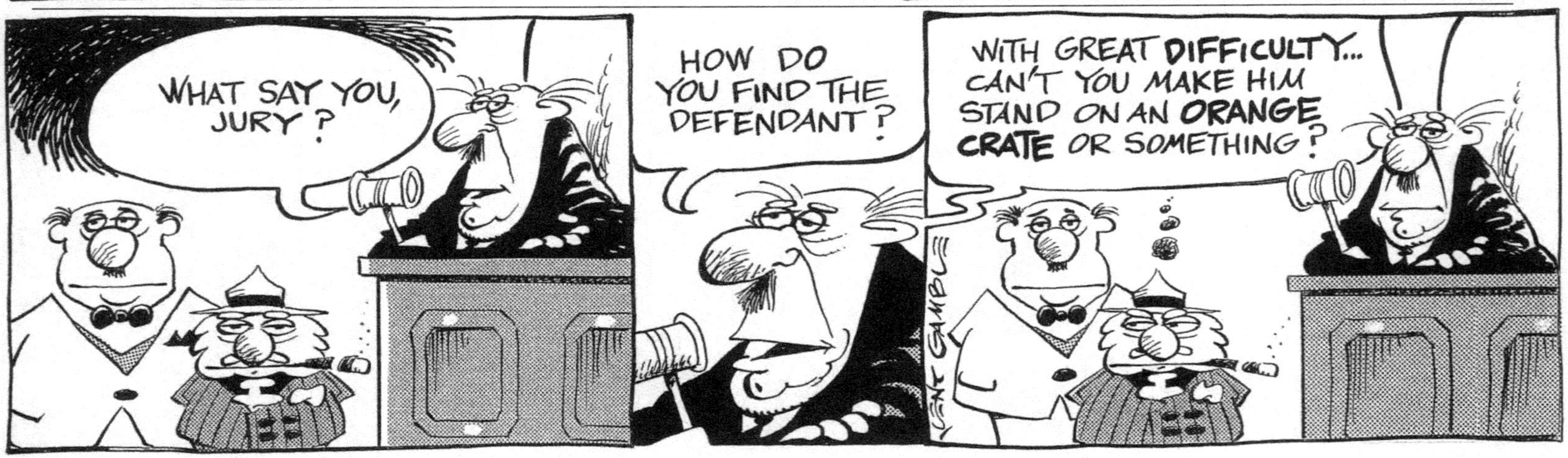
WHAT SAY YOU, JURY ?
HOW DO YOU FIND THE DEFENDANT ?
WITH GREAT DIFFICULTY... CAN'T YOU MAKE HIM STAND ON AN ORANGE CRATE OR SOMETHING ?
KENT GAMBLE

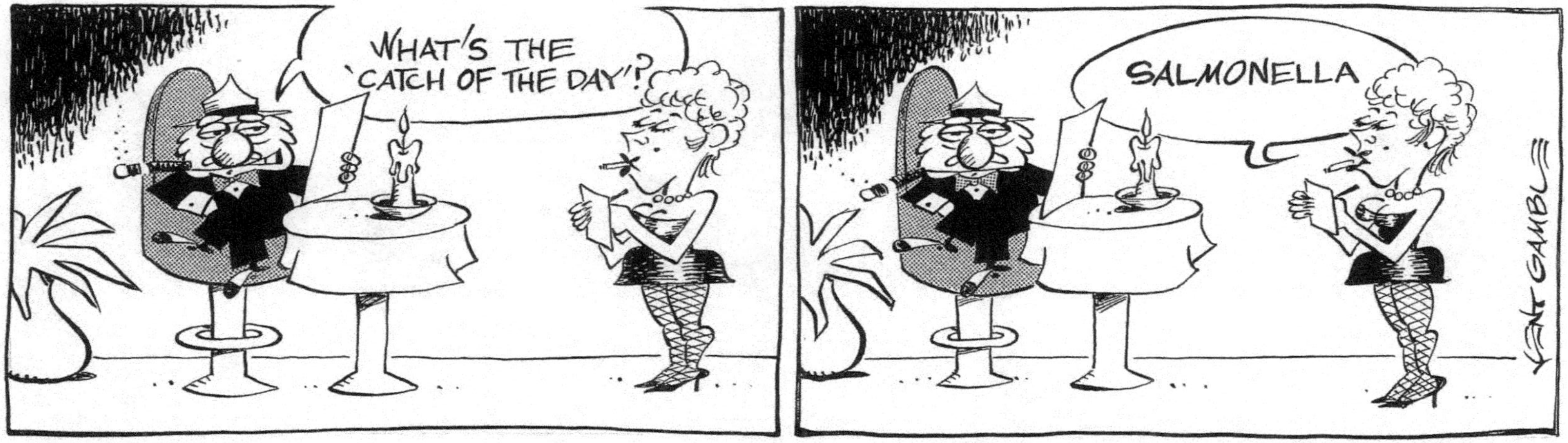
WHAT'S THE 'CATCH OF THE DAY'?
SALMONELLA
KENT GAMBLE

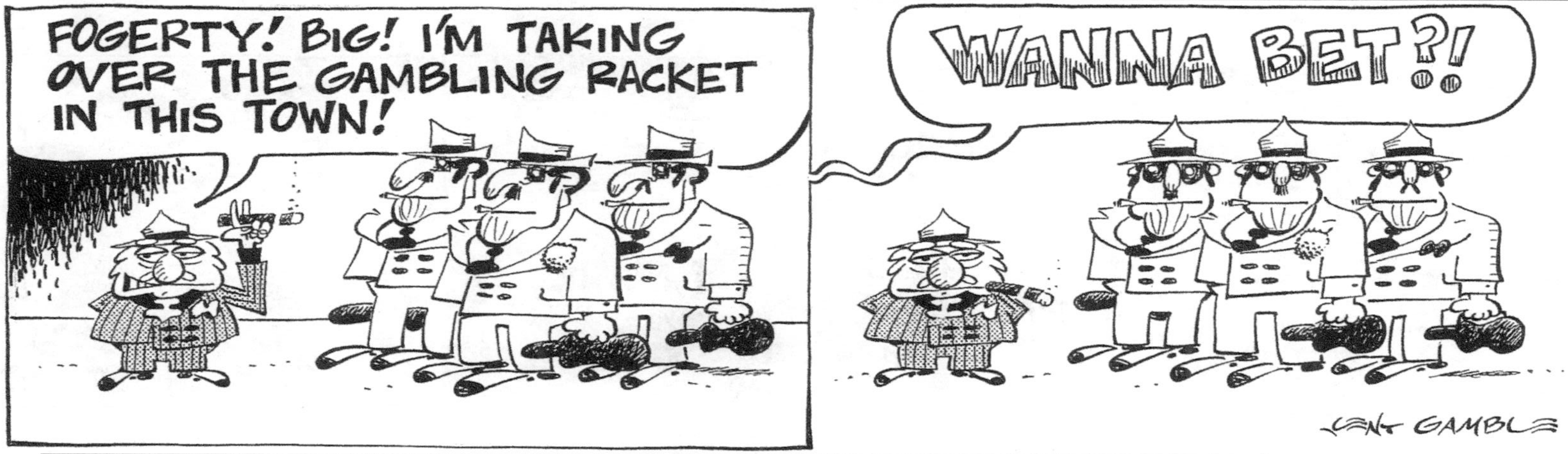
FOGERTY! BIG! I'M TAKING OVER THE GAMBLING RACKET IN THIS TOWN!
WANNA BET?!
KENT GAMBLE

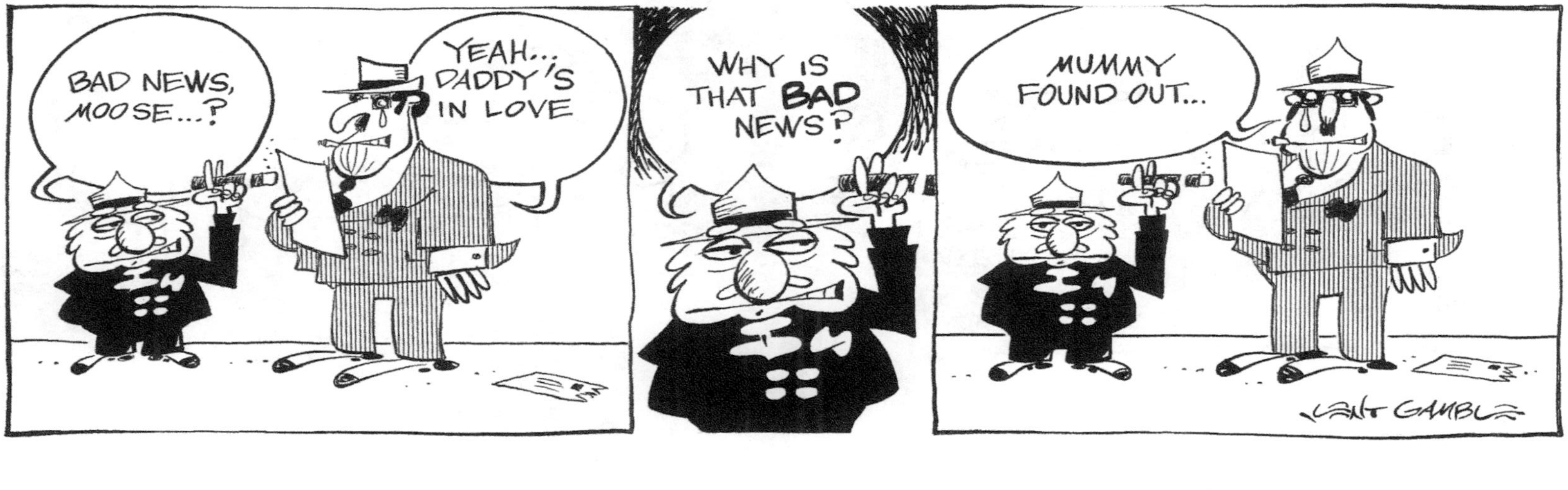
BAD NEWS, MOOSE...?
YEAH... DADDY'S IN LOVE
WHY IS THAT BAD NEWS?
MUMMY FOUND OUT...
KENT GAMBLE

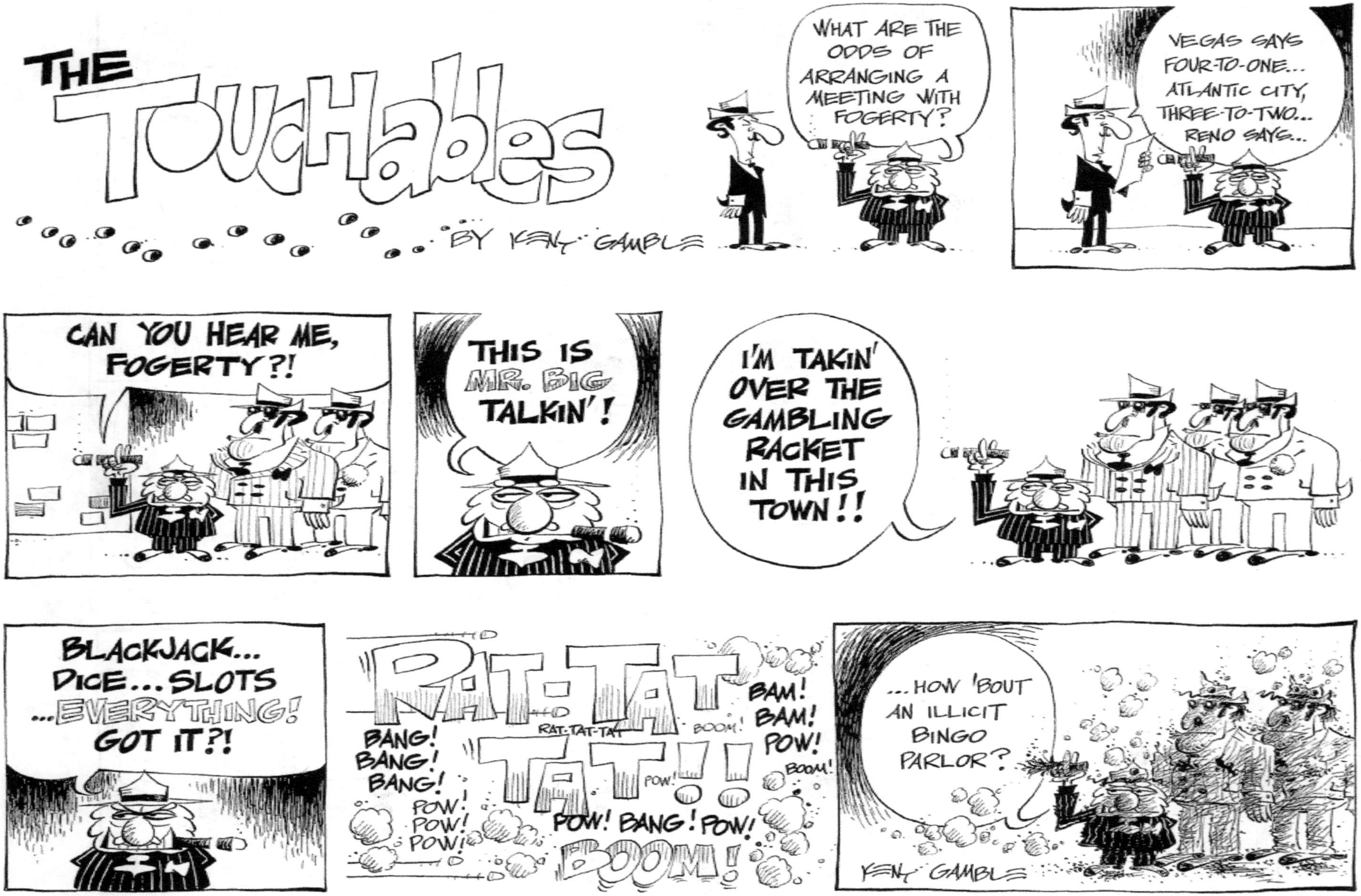
THE TOUCHABLES
BY KENT GAMBLE
WHAT ARE THE ODDS OF ARRANGING A MEETING WITH FOGERTY?
VEGAS SAYS FOUR-TO-ONE... ATLANTIC CITY, THREE-TO-TWO... RENO SAYS...
CAN YOU HEAR ME, FOGERTY?!
THIS IS MR. BIG TALKIN'!
I'M TAKIN' OVER THE GAMBLING RACKET IN THIS TOWN!!
BLACKJACK... DICE... SLOTS ...EVERYTHING! GOT IT?!
RAT-TAT-TAT!!
RAT-TAT-TAT
BANG! BANG! BANG!
POW! POW! POW!
BAM! BAM! POW!
BOOM!
BOOM!
POW!
POW! BANG! POW!
BOOM!
...HOW 'BOUT AN ILLICIT BINGO PARLOR?
KENT GAMBLE

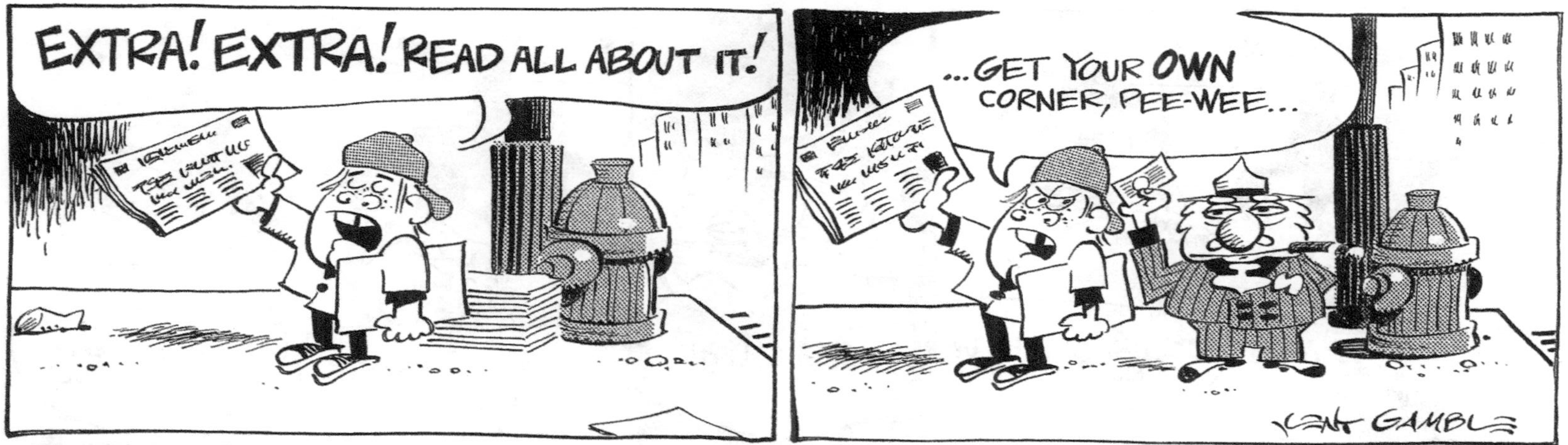
EXTRA! EXTRA! READ ALL ABOUT IT!
...GET YOUR OWN CORNER, PEE-WEE...
KENT GAMBLE

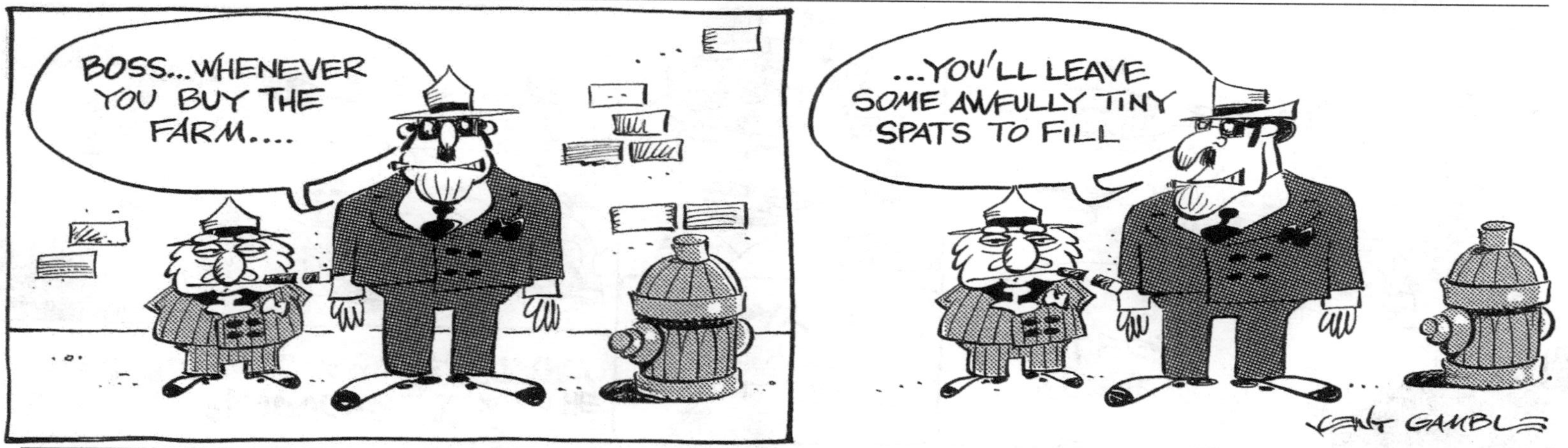
BOSS...WHENEVER YOU BUY THE FARM....
...YOU'LL LEAVE SOME AWFULLY TINY SPATS TO FILL
KENT GAMBLE

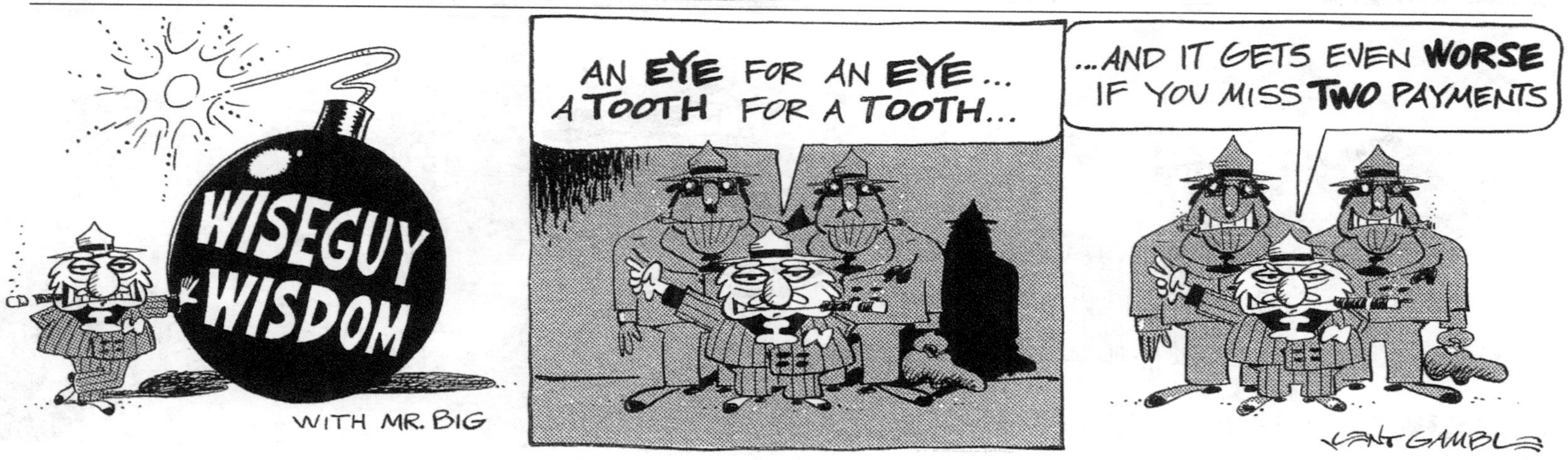
WISEGUY WISDOM
WITH MR. BIG
AN EYE FOR AN EYE... A TOOTH FOR A TOOTH...
...AND IT GETS EVEN WORSE IF YOU MISS TWO PAYMENTS
KENT GAMBLE

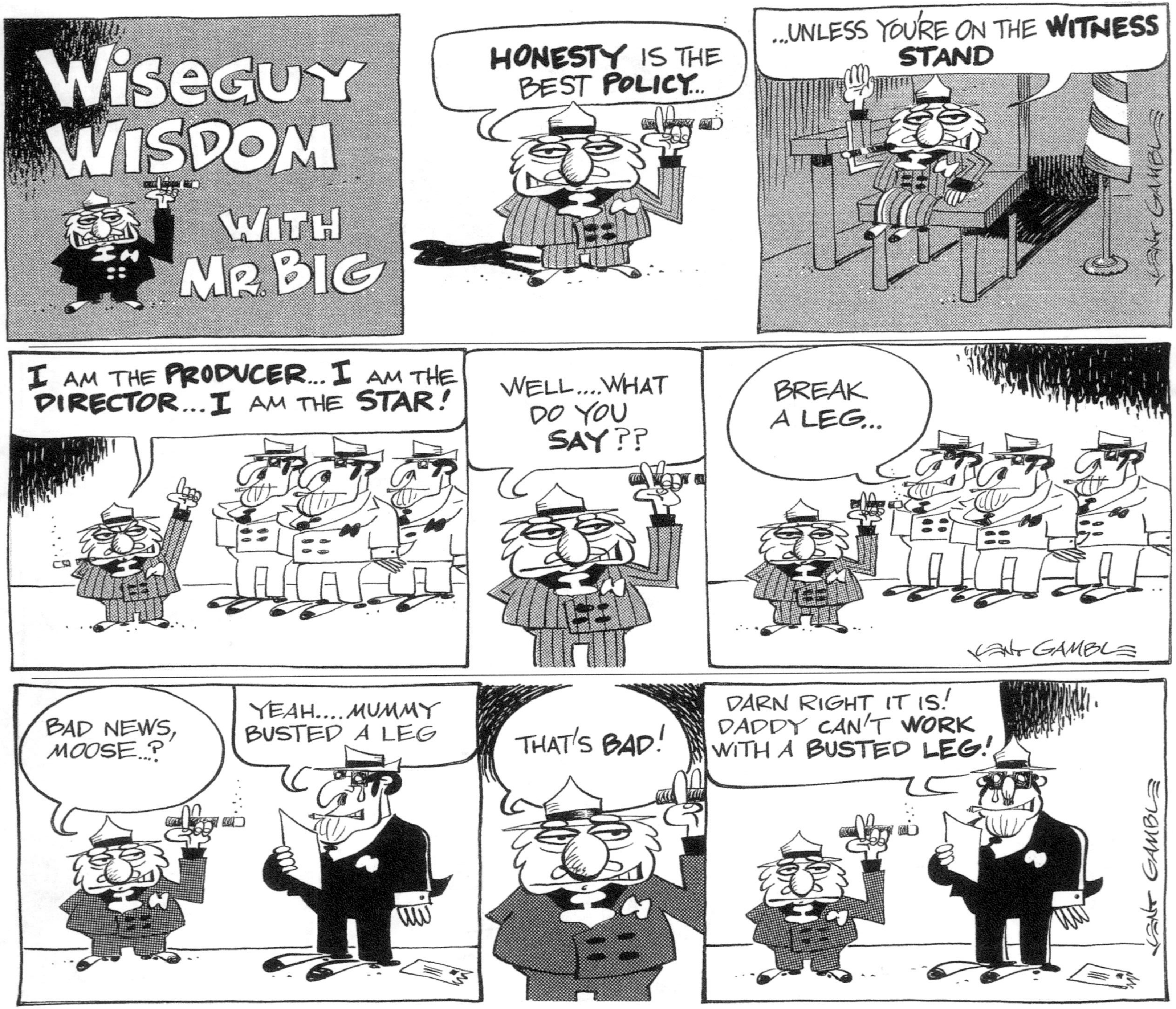
WISEGUY WISDOM WITH MR. BIG
HONESTY IS THE BEST POLICY...
...UNLESS YOU'RE ON THE WITNESS STAND
KENT GAMBLE
I AM THE PRODUCER... I AM THE DIRECTOR... I AM THE STAR!
WELL.... WHAT DO YOU SAY??
BREAK A LEG...
KENT GAMBLE
BAD NEWS, MOOSE...?
YEAH.... MUMMY BUSTED A LEG
THAT'S BAD!
DARN RIGHT IT IS! DADDY CAN'T WORK WITH A BUSTED LEG!
KENT GAMBLE

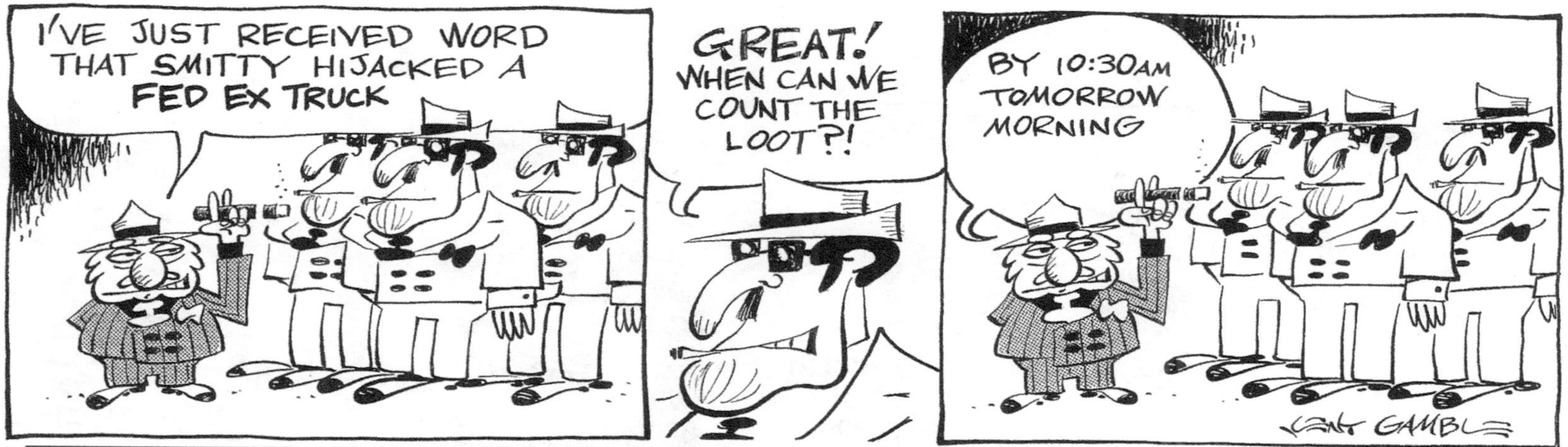
I'VE JUST RECEIVED WORD THAT SMITTY HIJACKED A FED EX TRUCK
GREAT! WHEN CAN WE COUNT THE LOOT?!
BY 10:30AM TOMORROW MORNING
KENT GAMBLE

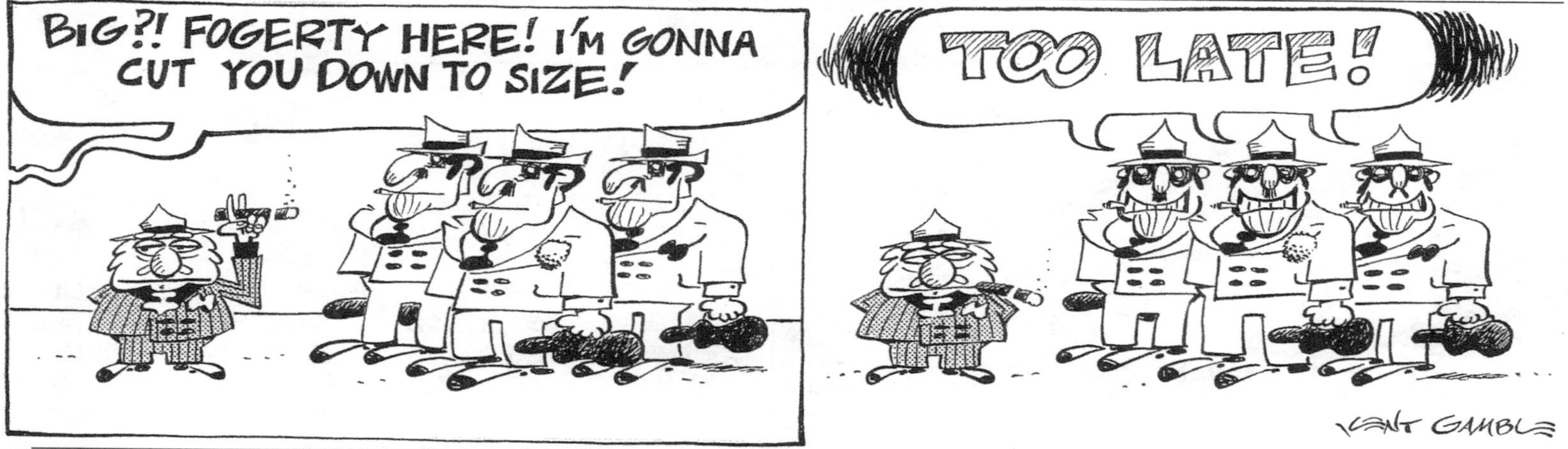
BIG?! FOGERTY HERE! I'M GONNA CUT YOU DOWN TO SIZE!
TOO LATE!
KENT GAMBLE

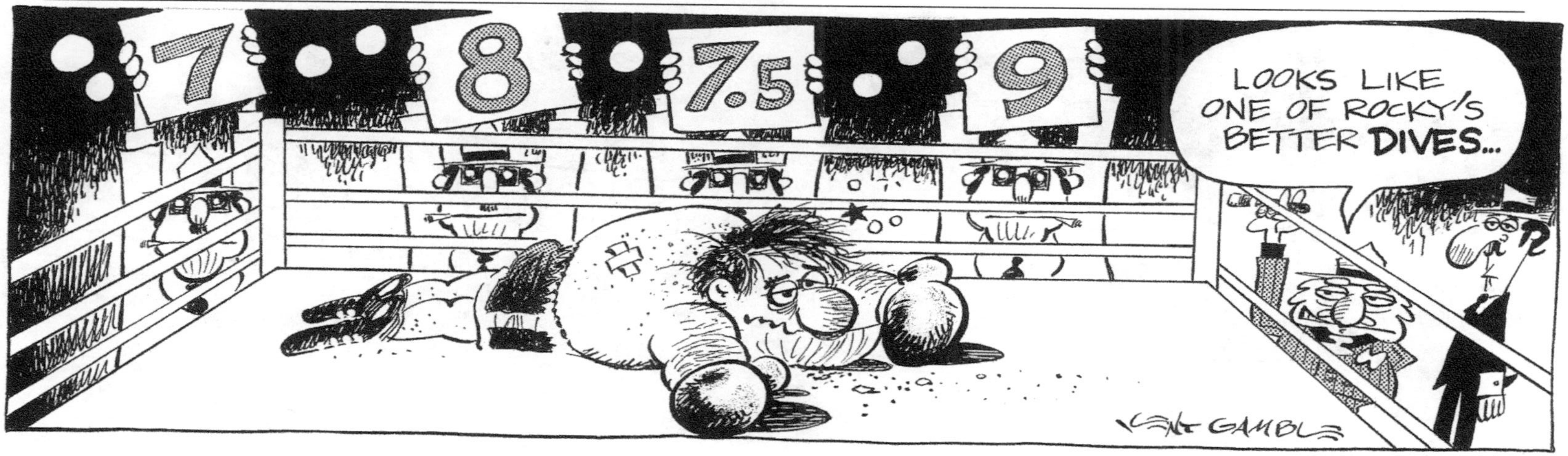
7
8
7.5
9
LOOKS LIKE ONE OF ROCKY'S BETTER DIVES...
KENT GAMBLE

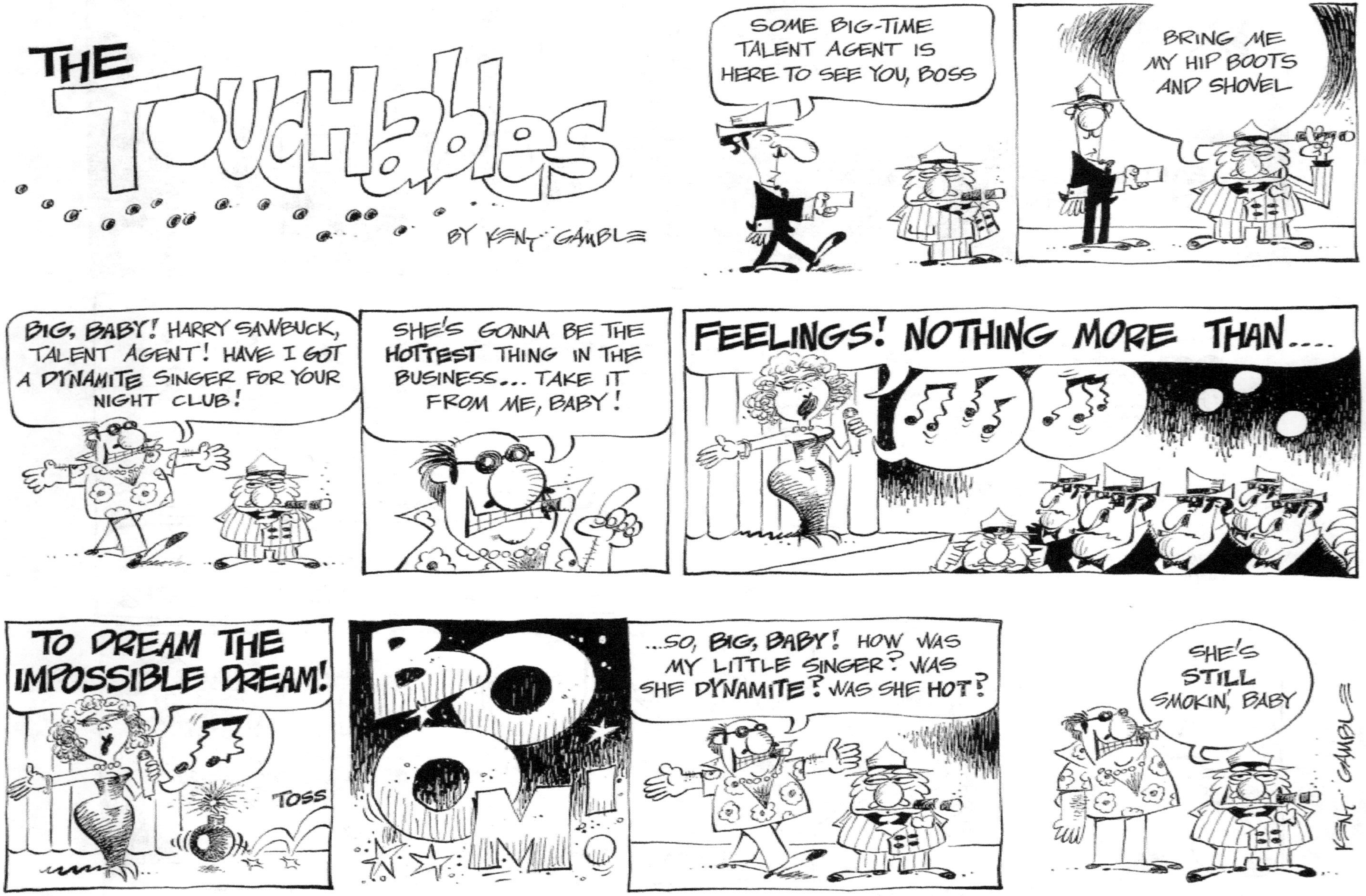
THE TOUCHABLES
BY KENT GAMBLE
SOME BIG-TIME TALENT AGENT IS HERE TO SEE YOU, BOSS
BRING ME MY HIP BOOTS AND SHOVEL
BIG, BABY! HARRY SAWBUCK, TALENT AGENT! HAVE I GOT A DYNAMITE SINGER FOR YOUR NIGHT CLUB!
SHE'S GONNA BE THE HOTTEST THING IN THE BUSINESS... TAKE IT FROM ME, BABY!
FEELINGS! NOTHING MORE THAN....
TO DREAM THE IMPOSSIBLE DREAM!
TOSS
BOOM!
...SO, BIG, BABY! HOW WAS MY LITTLE SINGER? WAS SHE DYNAMITE? WAS SHE HOT?
SHE'S STILL SMOKIN', BABY
KENT GAMBLE

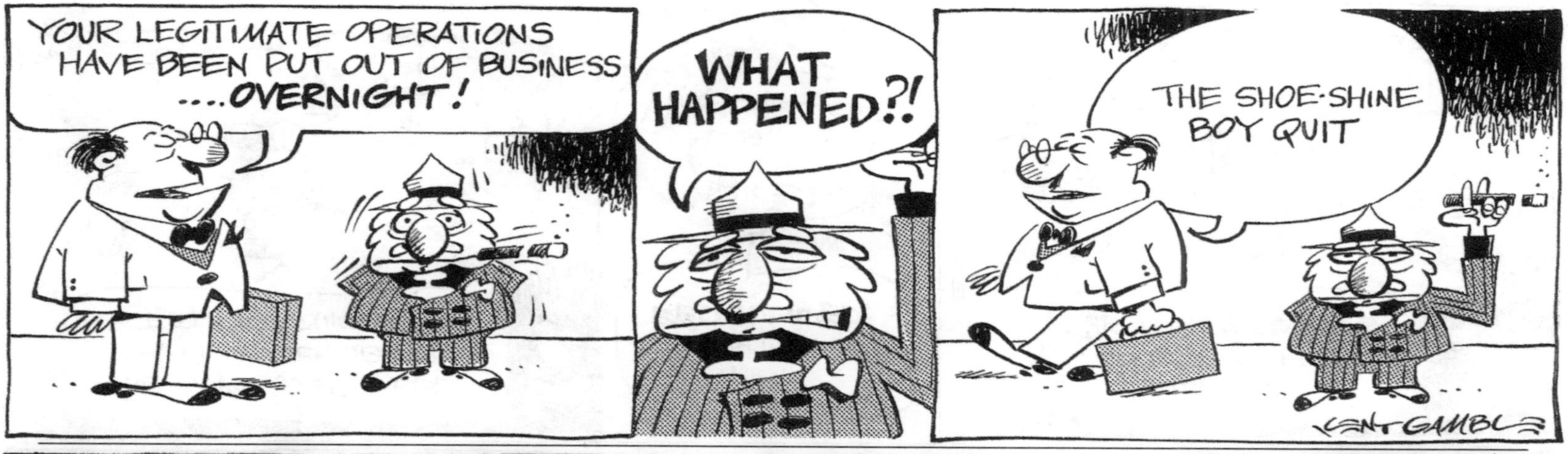
YOUR LEGITIMATE OPERATIONS HAVE BEEN PUT OUT OF BUSINESS ....OVERNIGHT!
WHAT HAPPENED?!
THE SHOE-SHINE BOY QUIT
KENT GAMBLE

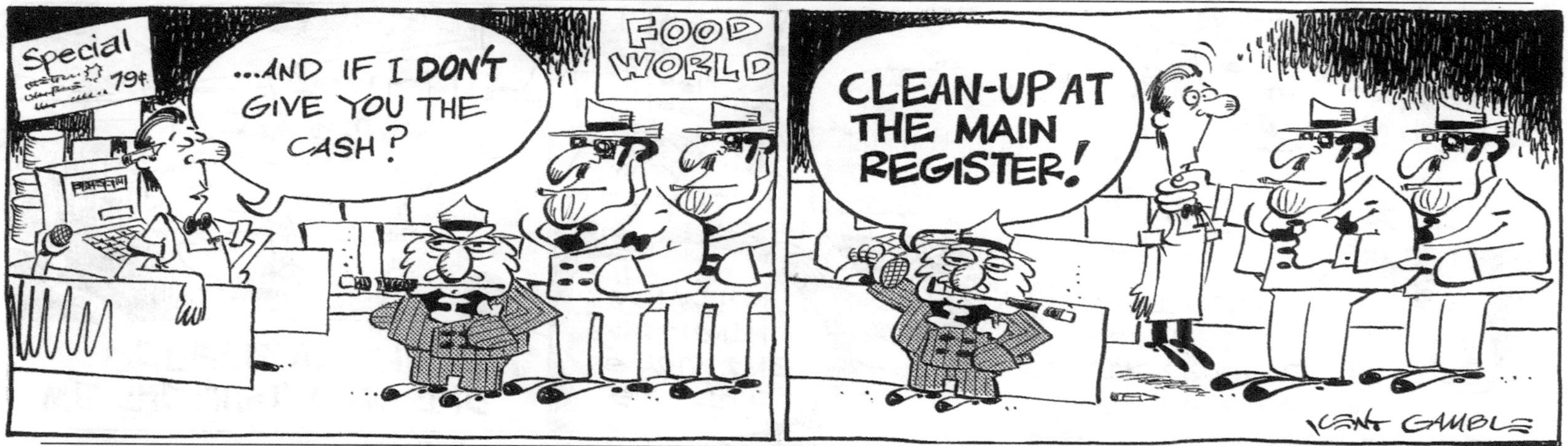
Special
79¢
...AND IF I DON'T GIVE YOU THE CASH?
FOOD WORLD
CLEAN-UP AT THE MAIN REGISTER!
KENT GAMBLE

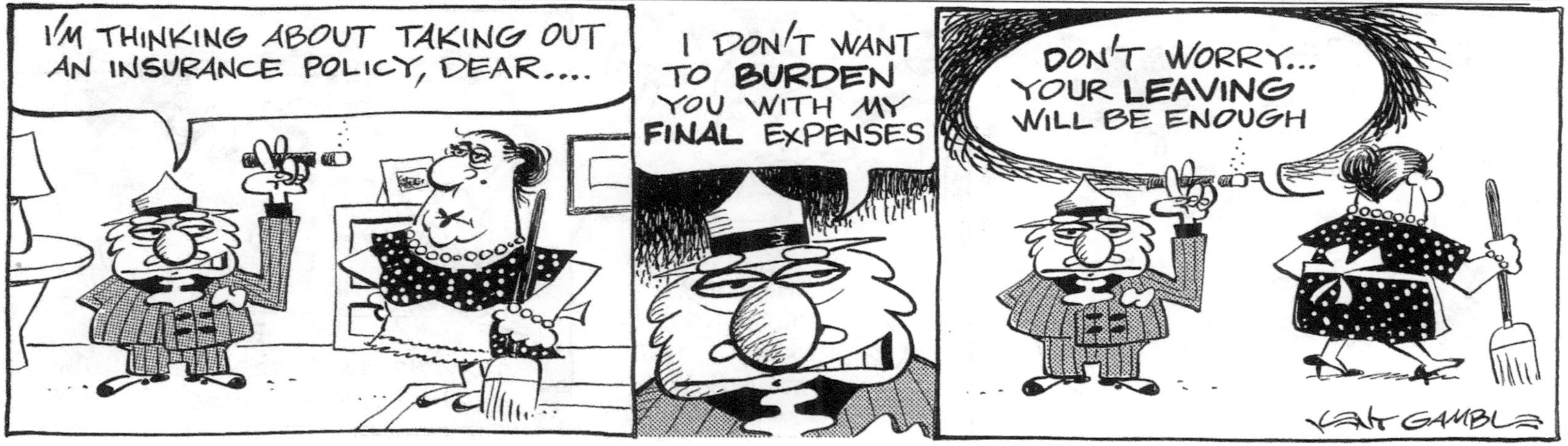
I'M THINKING ABOUT TAKING OUT AN INSURANCE POLICY, DEAR....
I DON'T WANT TO BURDEN YOU WITH MY FINAL EXPENSES
DON'T WORRY... YOUR LEAVING WILL BE ENOUGH
KENT GAMBLE

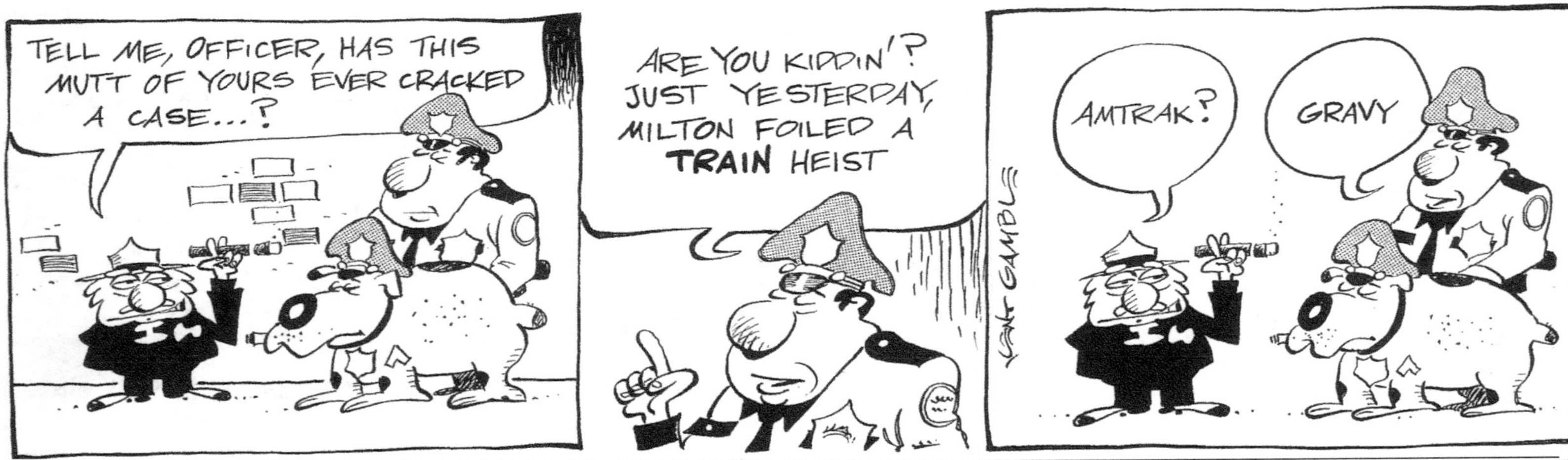
TELL ME, OFFICER, HAS THIS MUTT OF YOURS EVER CRACKED A CASE...?
ARE YOU KIDDIN'? JUST YESTERDAY, MILTON FOILED A **TRAIN** HEIST
AMTRAK?
GRAVY
KENT GAMBLE

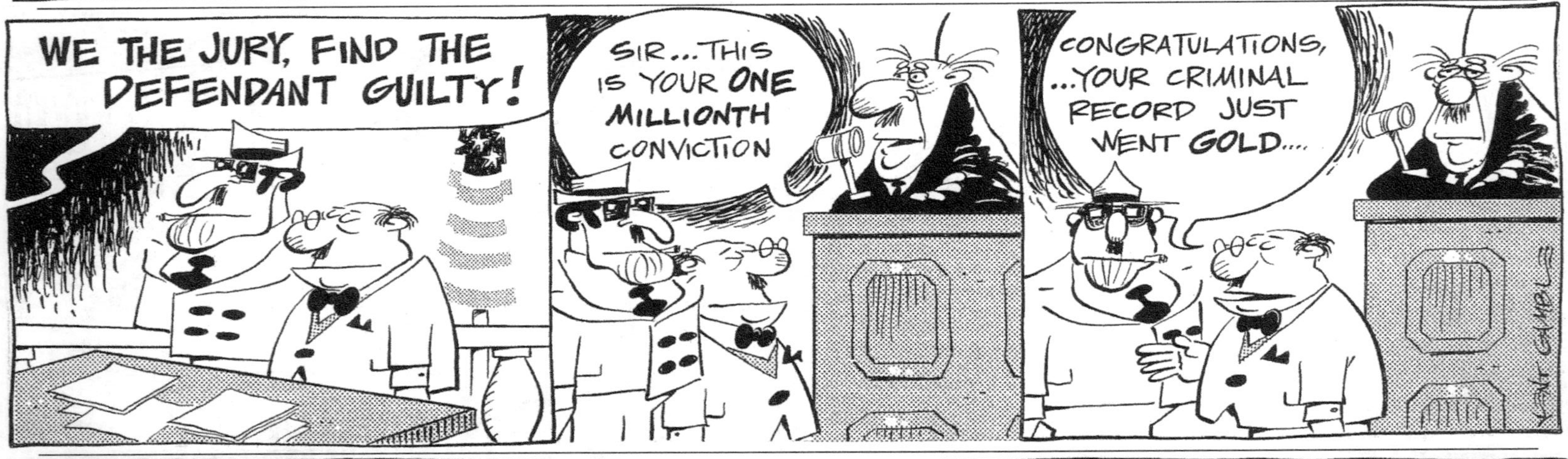
WE THE JURY, FIND THE DEFENDANT GUILTY!
SIR...THIS IS YOUR **ONE MILLIONTH** CONVICTION
CONGRATULATIONS, ...YOUR CRIMINAL RECORD JUST WENT **GOLD**....
KENT GAMBLE

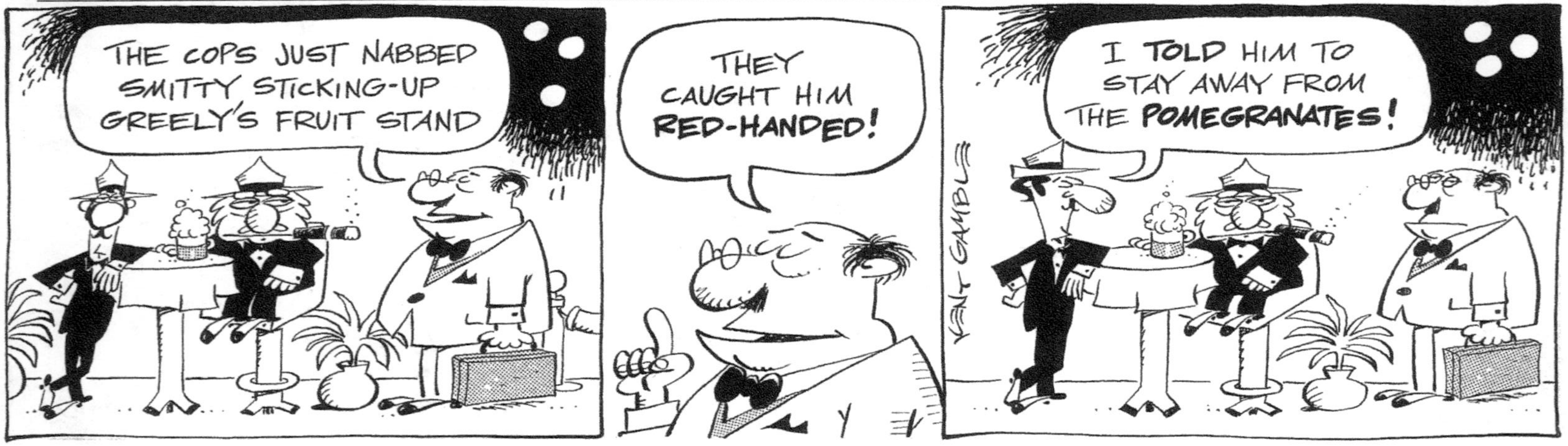
THE COPS JUST NABBED SMITTY STICKING-UP GREELY'S FRUIT STAND
THEY CAUGHT HIM **RED-HANDED**!
I **TOLD** HIM TO STAY AWAY FROM THE **POMEGRANATES**!
KENT GAMBLE

I'LL HAVE THE STEAK AND LOBSTER, TOOTS...
...OH, AND BRING ME A SHRIMP COCKTAIL FOR STARTERS
STRAIGHT UP OR ON THE ROCKS?
KENT GAMBLE

ARE YOU STILL WORRIED ABOUT THAT SILLY DENTAL CHECK-UP?
WHAT COULD A DENTIST POSSIBLY SAY TO SCARE YOU?
LOOKS LIKE WE'LL HAVE TO AMPUTATE...
KENT GAMBLE

THIS ONE HELD A REVOLVER ON ME, WHILE THAT ONE CLEANED OUT MY STORE!
WELL...WHAT DO YOU HAVE TO SAY FOR YOURSELVES?
CERTAINLY YOUR HONOR HAS HEARD OF REVOLVING CREDIT
KENT GAMBLE

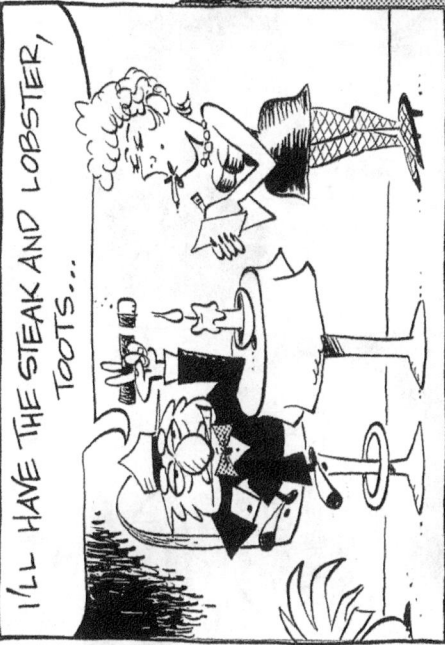

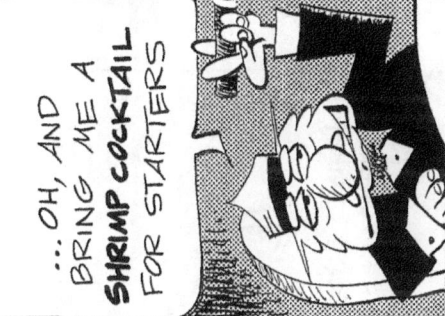

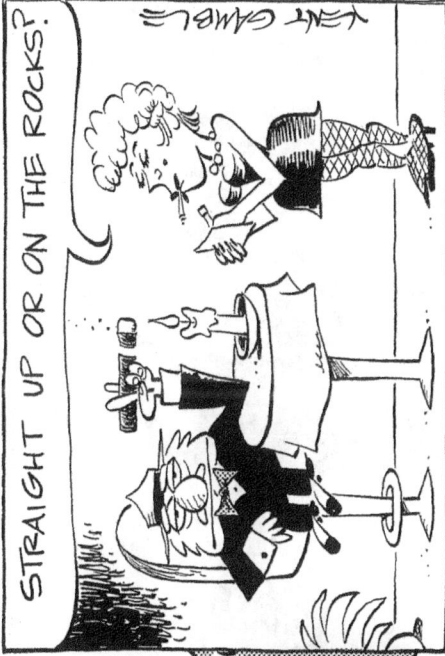

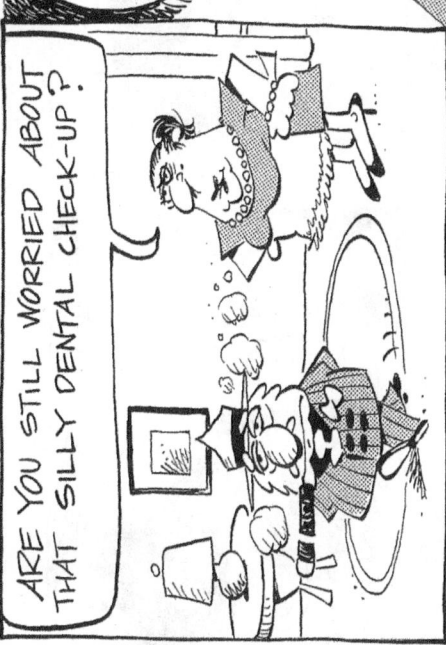

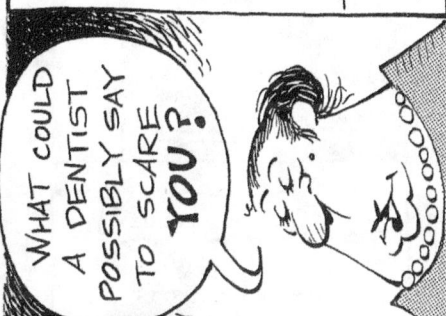

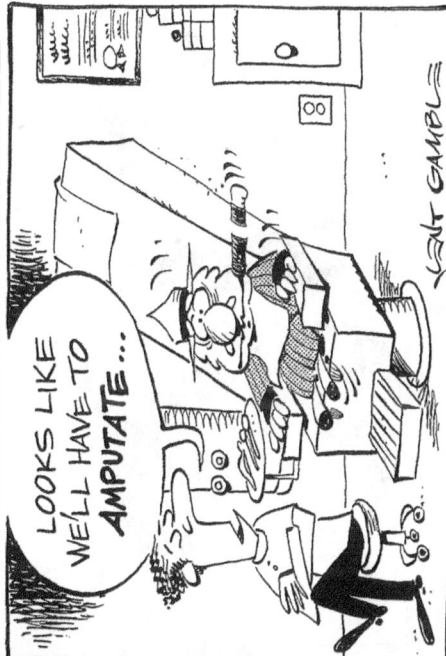

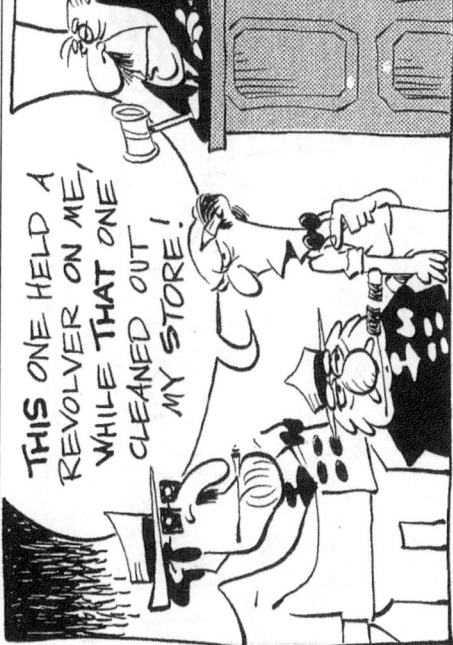

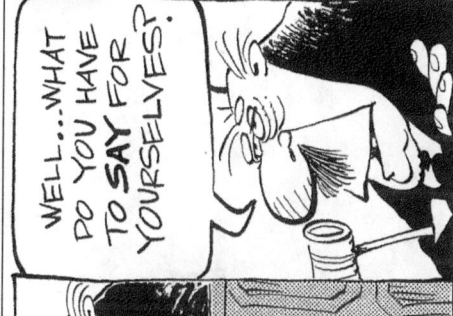

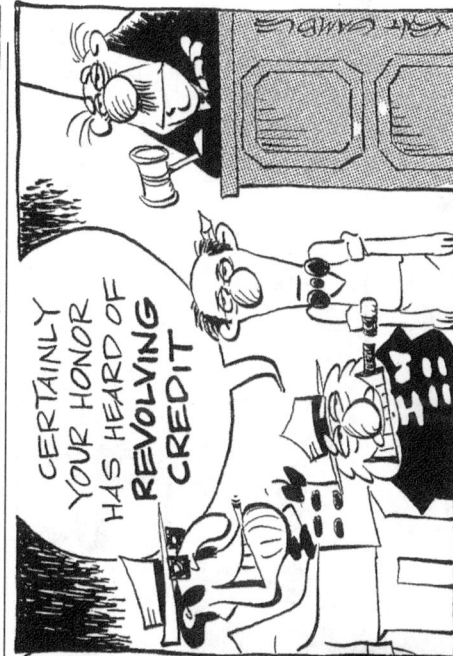

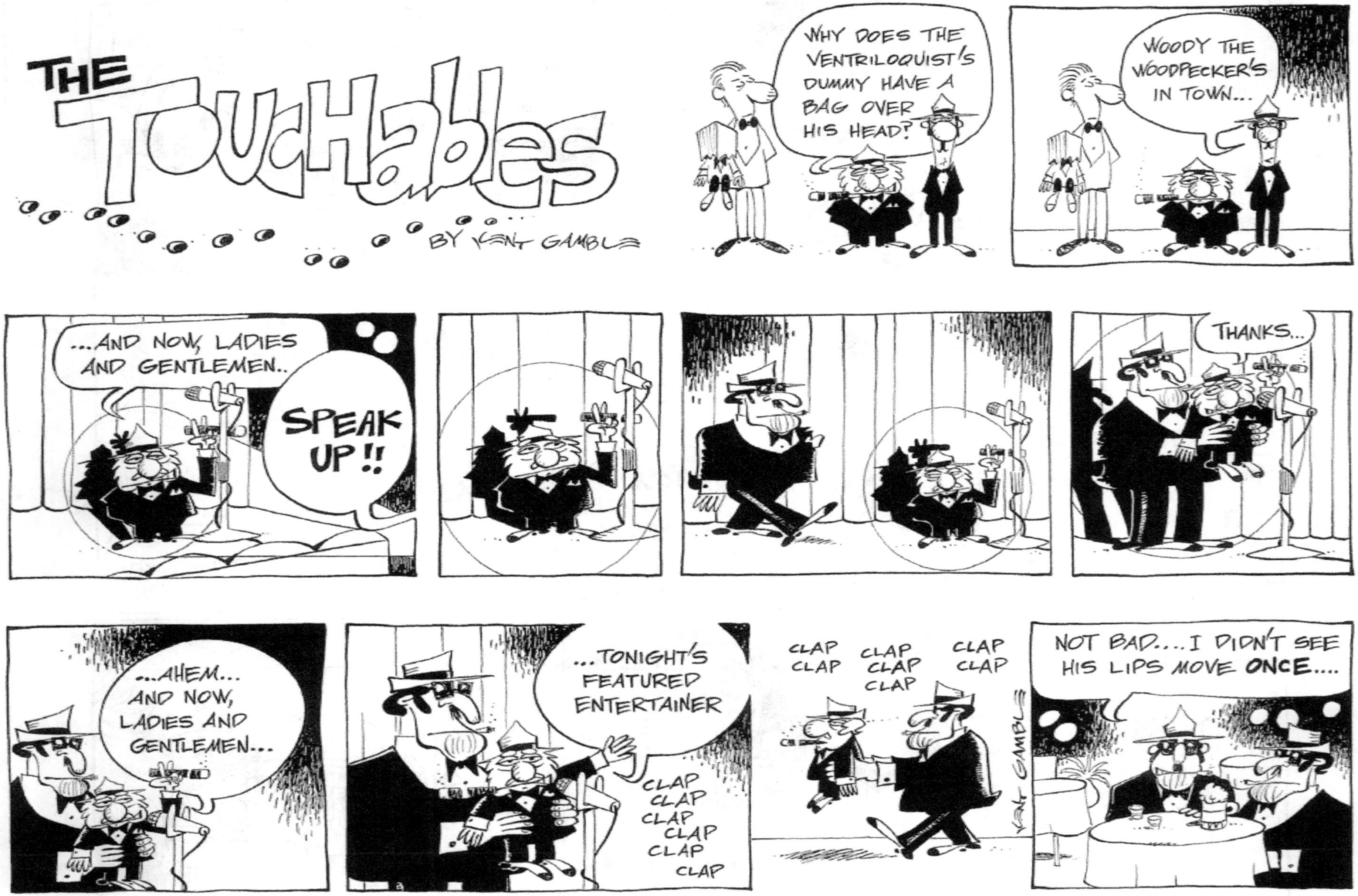
THE TOUCHABLES
BY KENT GAMBLE
WHY DOES THE VENTRILOQUIST'S DUMMY HAVE A BAG OVER HIS HEAD?
WOODY THE WOODPECKER'S IN TOWN...
...AND NOW, LADIES AND GENTLEMEN..
SPEAK UP!!
THANKS...
...AHEM... AND NOW, LADIES AND GENTLEMEN...
...TONIGHT'S FEATURED ENTERTAINER
CLAP CLAP CLAP CLAP CLAP CLAP
CLAP CLAP
CLAP CLAP CLAP
CLAP CLAP
KENT GAMBLE
NOT BAD.... I DIDN'T SEE HIS LIPS MOVE ONCE....

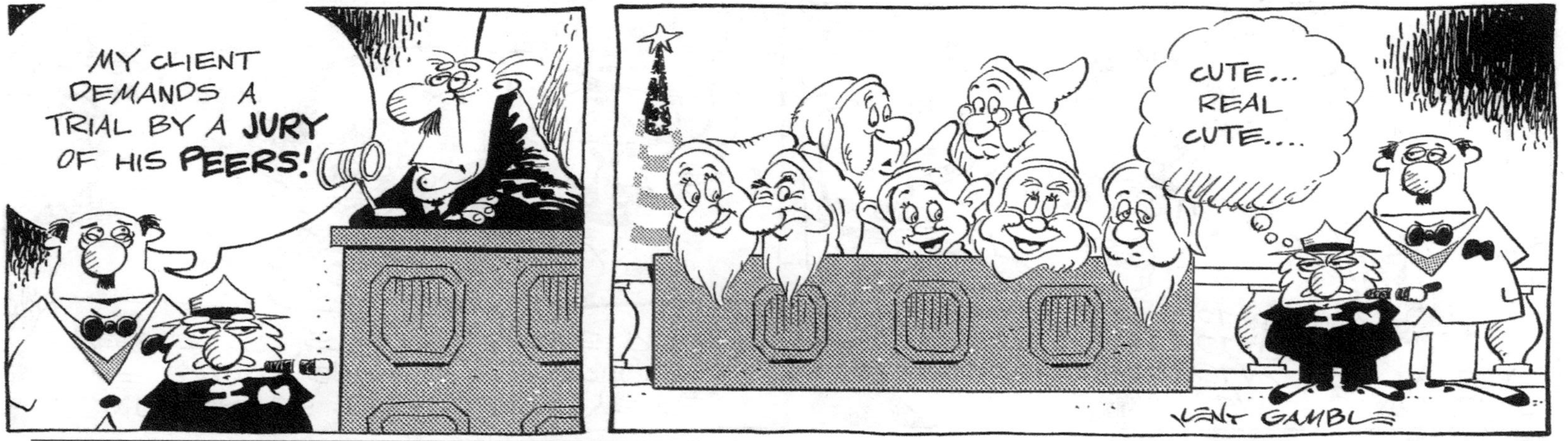
MY CLIENT DEMANDS A TRIAL BY A **JURY** OF HIS **PEERS!**
CUTE... REAL CUTE....
KENT GAMBLE

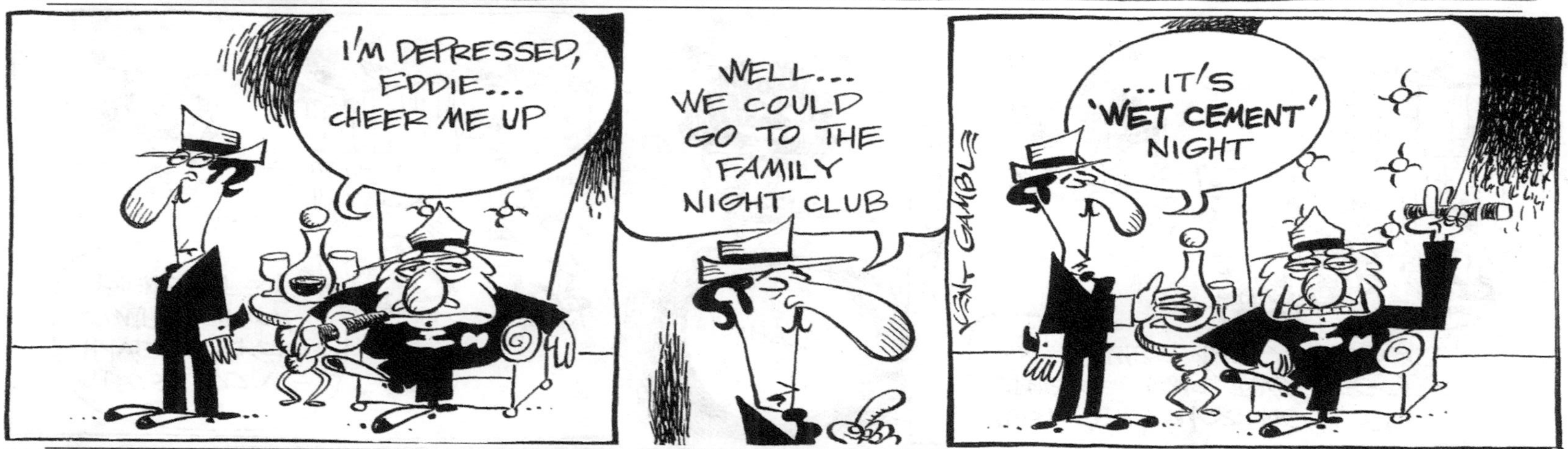
I'M DEPRESSED, EDDIE... CHEER ME UP
WELL... WE COULD GO TO THE FAMILY NIGHT CLUB
...IT'S **'WET CEMENT'** NIGHT
KENT GAMBLE

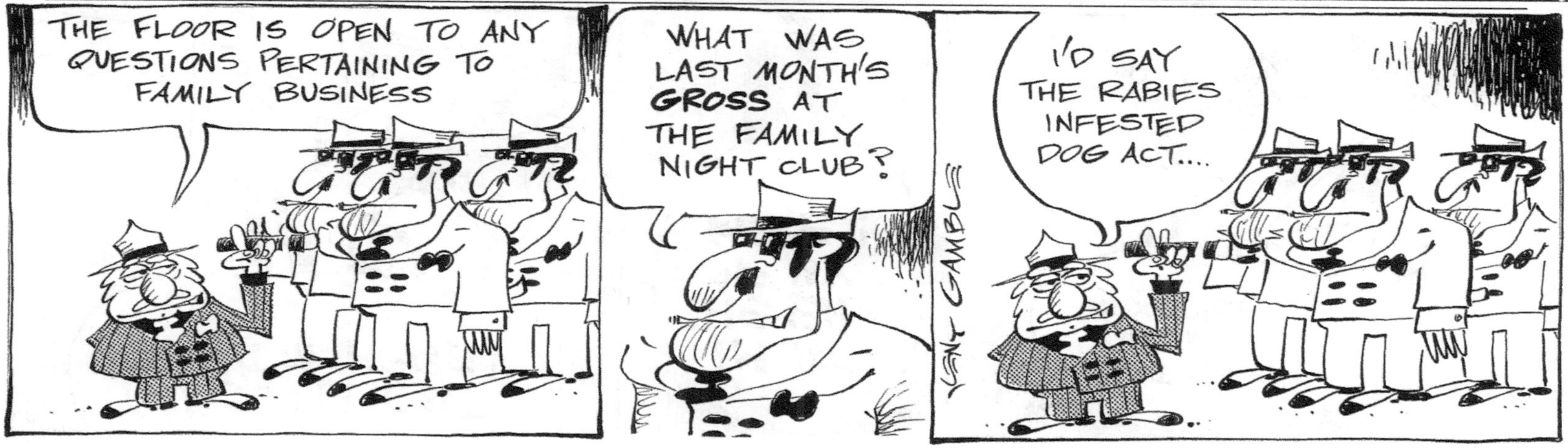
THE FLOOR IS OPEN TO ANY QUESTIONS PERTAINING TO FAMILY BUSINESS
WHAT WAS LAST MONTH'S **GROSS** AT THE FAMILY NIGHT CLUB?
I'D SAY THE RABIES INFESTED DOG ACT....
KENT GAMBLE

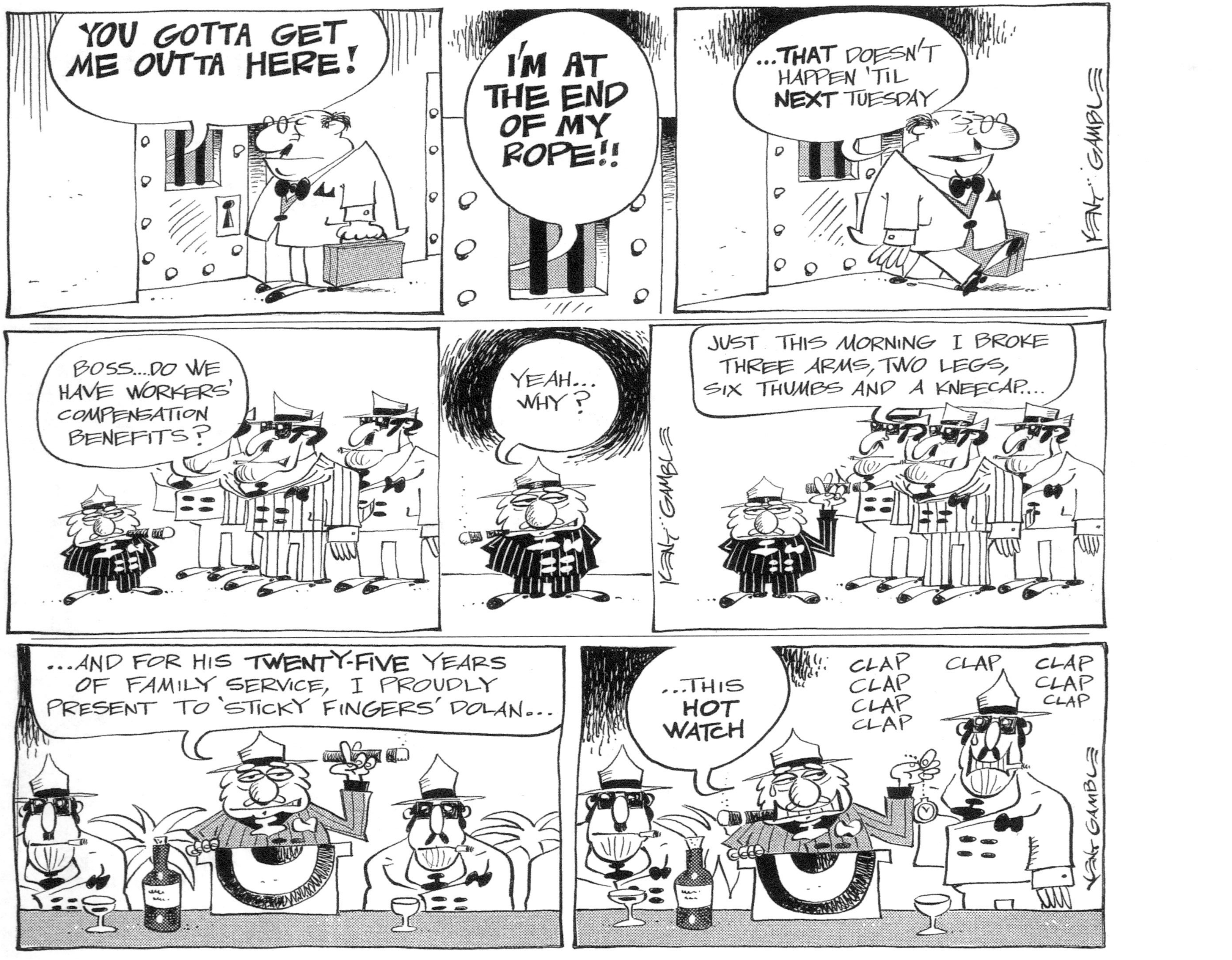
YOU GOTTA GET ME OUTTA HERE!
I'M AT THE END OF MY ROPE!!
...THAT DOESN'T HAPPEN 'TIL NEXT TUESDAY
KENT GAMBLE
BOSS...DO WE HAVE WORKERS' COMPENSATION BENEFITS?
YEAH... WHY?
KENT GAMBLE
JUST THIS MORNING I BROKE THREE ARMS, TWO LEGS, SIX THUMBS AND A KNEECAP...
...AND FOR HIS TWENTY-FIVE YEARS OF FAMILY SERVICE, I PROUDLY PRESENT TO 'STICKY FINGERS' DOLAN...
...THIS HOT WATCH
CLAP CLAP CLAP CLAP
CLAP
CLAP CLAP CLAP
KENT GAMBLE

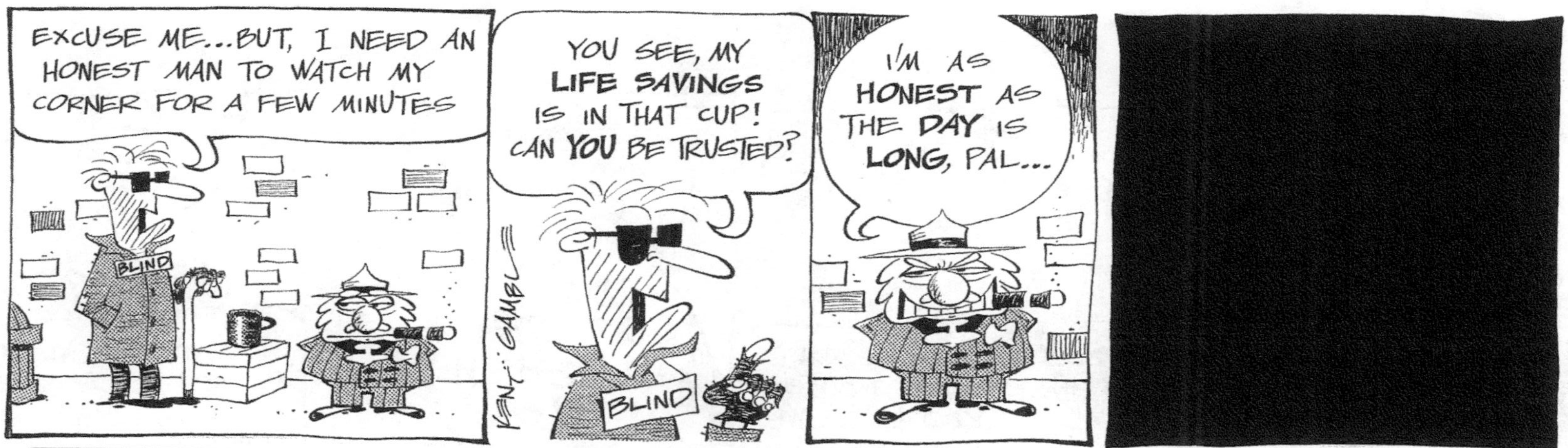
EXCUSE ME...BUT, I NEED AN HONEST MAN TO WATCH MY CORNER FOR A FEW MINUTES
BLIND
YOU SEE, MY **LIFE SAVINGS** IS IN THAT CUP! CAN **YOU** BE TRUSTED?
BLIND
I'M AS **HONEST** AS THE **DAY** IS **LONG**, PAL...
KENT GAMBLE

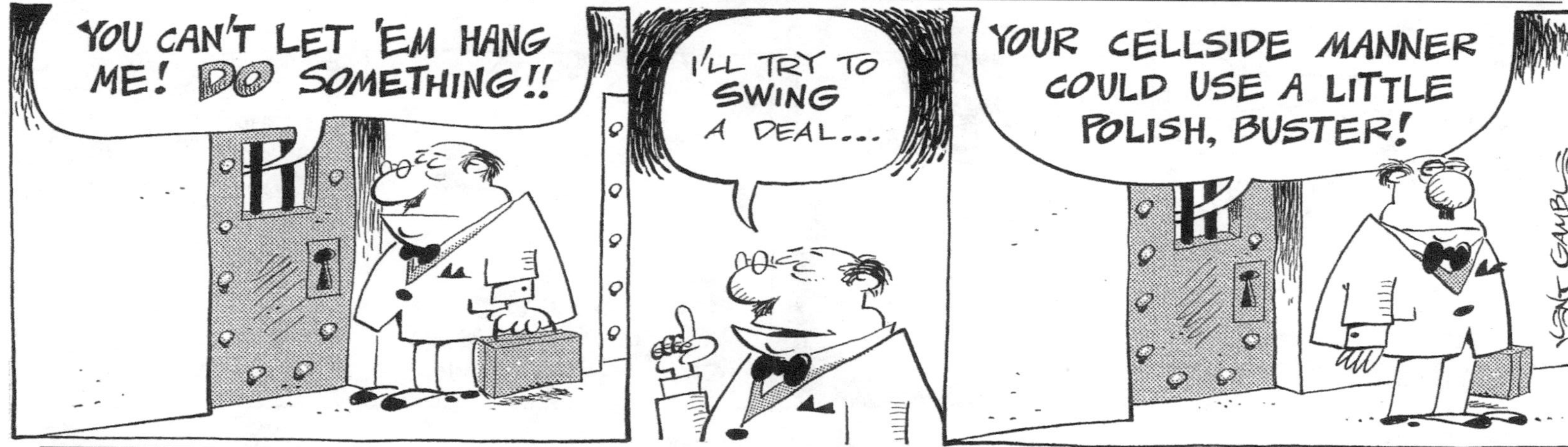
YOU CAN'T LET 'EM HANG ME! **DO** SOMETHING!!
I'LL TRY TO **SWING** A DEAL...
YOUR CELLSIDE MANNER COULD USE A LITTLE POLISH, BUSTER!
KENT GAMBLE

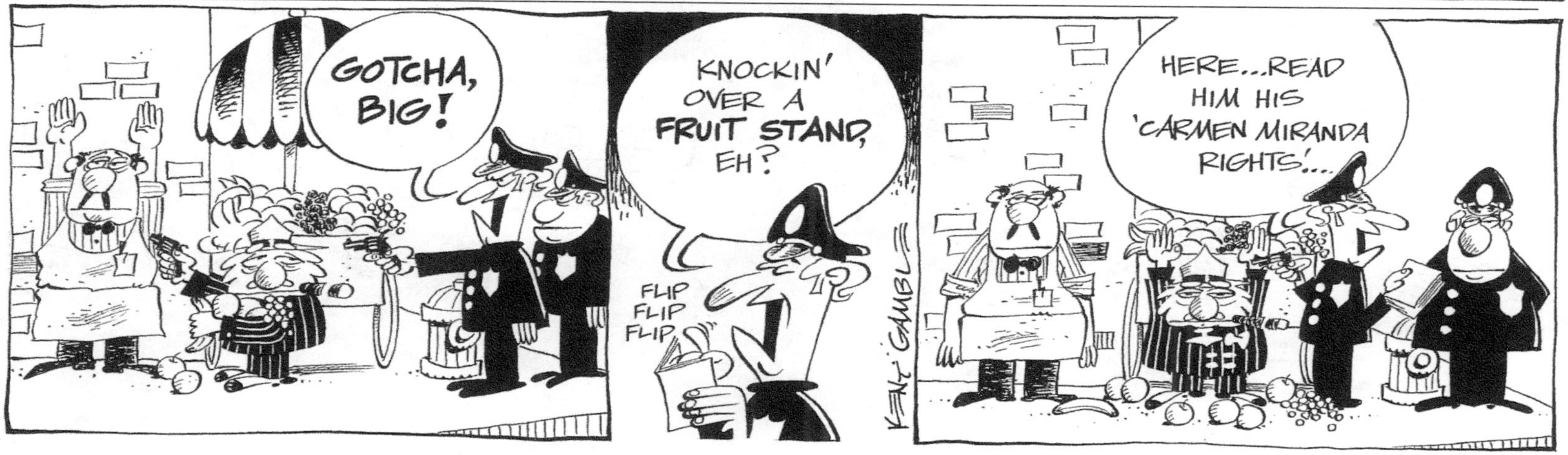
GOTCHA, BIG!
KNOCKIN' OVER A **FRUIT STAND**, EH?
FLIP FLIP FLIP
KENT GAMBLE
HERE...READ HIM HIS 'CARMEN MIRANDA RIGHTS'...

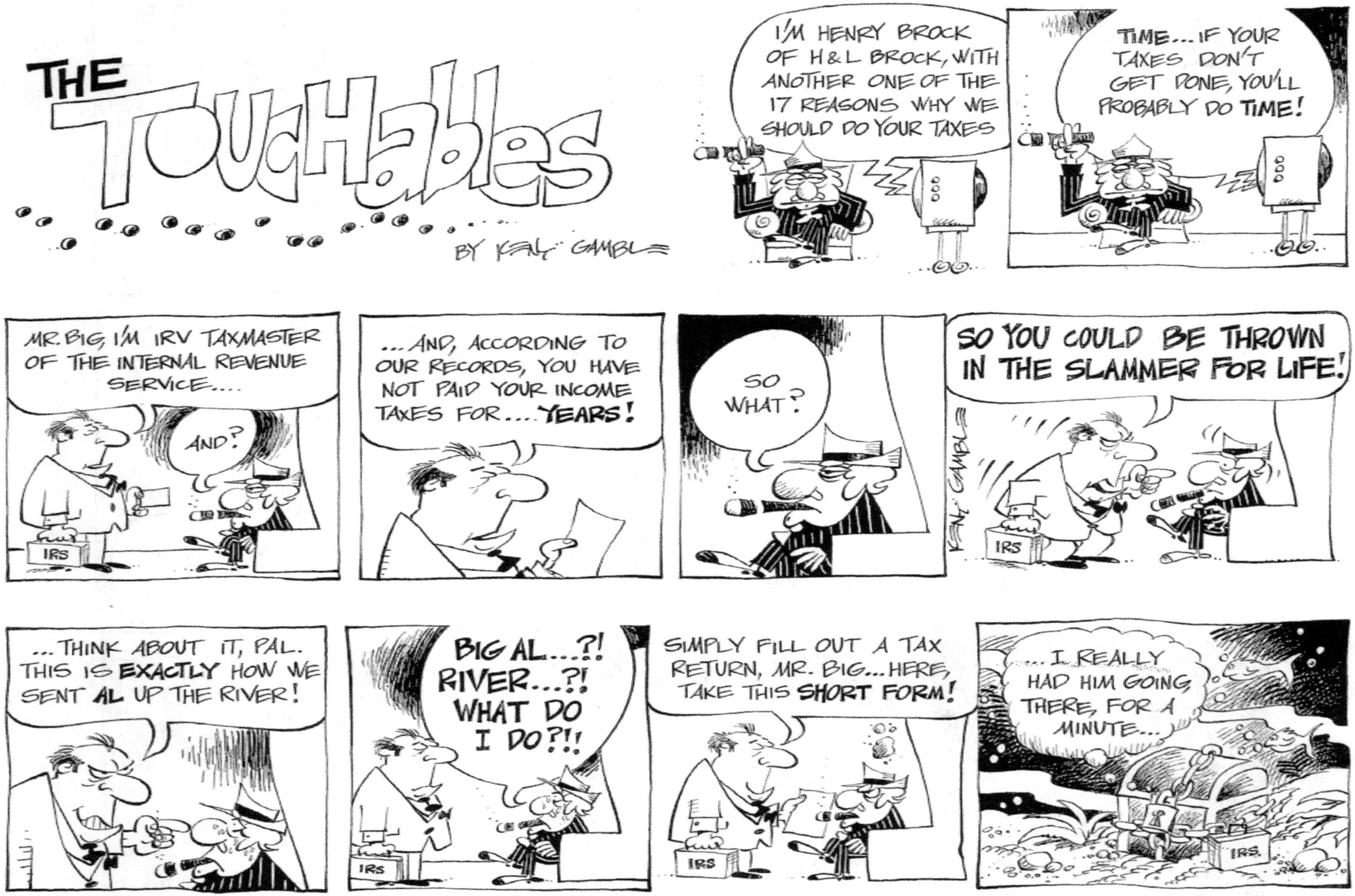
THE TOUCHABLES
BY KEN GAMBLE
I'M HENRY BROCK OF H&L BROCK, WITH ANOTHER ONE OF THE 17 REASONS WHY WE SHOULD DO YOUR TAXES
TIME... IF YOUR TAXES DON'T GET DONE, YOU'LL PROBABLY DO TIME!
MR. BIG, I'M IRV TAXMASTER OF THE INTERNAL REVENUE SERVICE....
AND?
IRS
...AND, ACCORDING TO OUR RECORDS, YOU HAVE NOT PAID YOUR INCOME TAXES FOR.... YEARS!
SO WHAT?
SO YOU COULD BE THROWN IN THE SLAMMER FOR LIFE!
IRS
...THINK ABOUT IT, PAL. THIS IS EXACTLY HOW WE SENT AL UP THE RIVER!
BIG AL...?! RIVER...?! WHAT DO I DO?!!
IRS
SIMPLY FILL OUT A TAX RETURN, MR. BIG... HERE, TAKE THIS SHORT FORM!
IRS
...I REALLY HAD HIM GOING THERE, FOR A MINUTE...
IRS

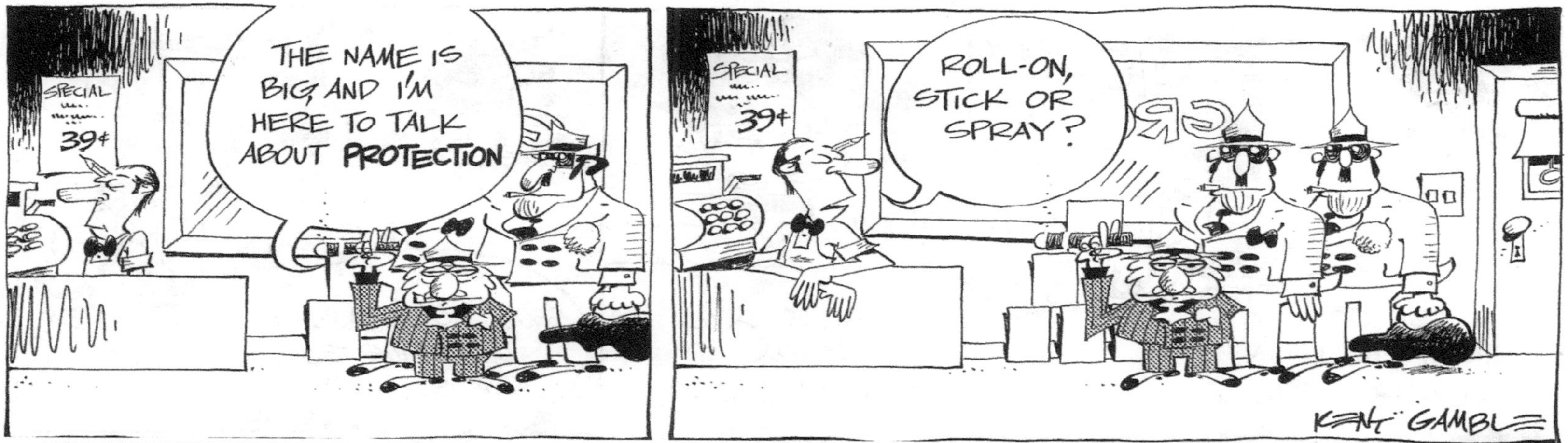
SPECIAL
39¢
THE NAME IS BIG AND I'M HERE TO TALK ABOUT PROTECTION
SPECIAL
39¢
ROLL-ON, STICK OR SPRAY?
KENT GAMBLE

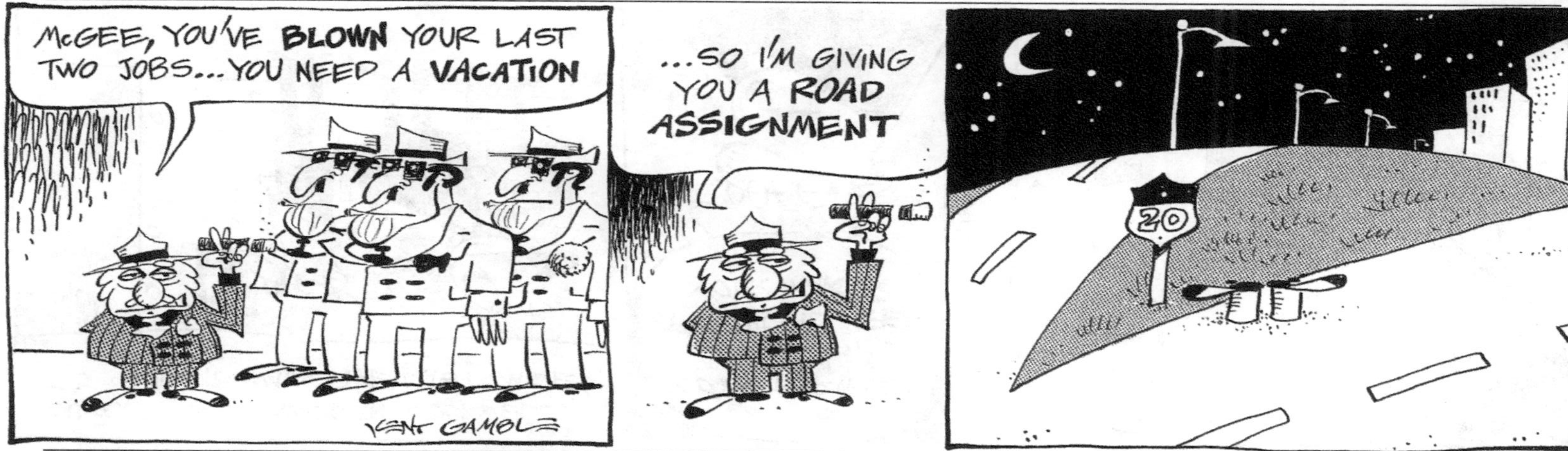
McGEE, YOU'VE BLOWN YOUR LAST TWO JOBS... YOU NEED A VACATION
KENT GAMBLE
...SO I'M GIVING YOU A ROAD ASSIGNMENT
20

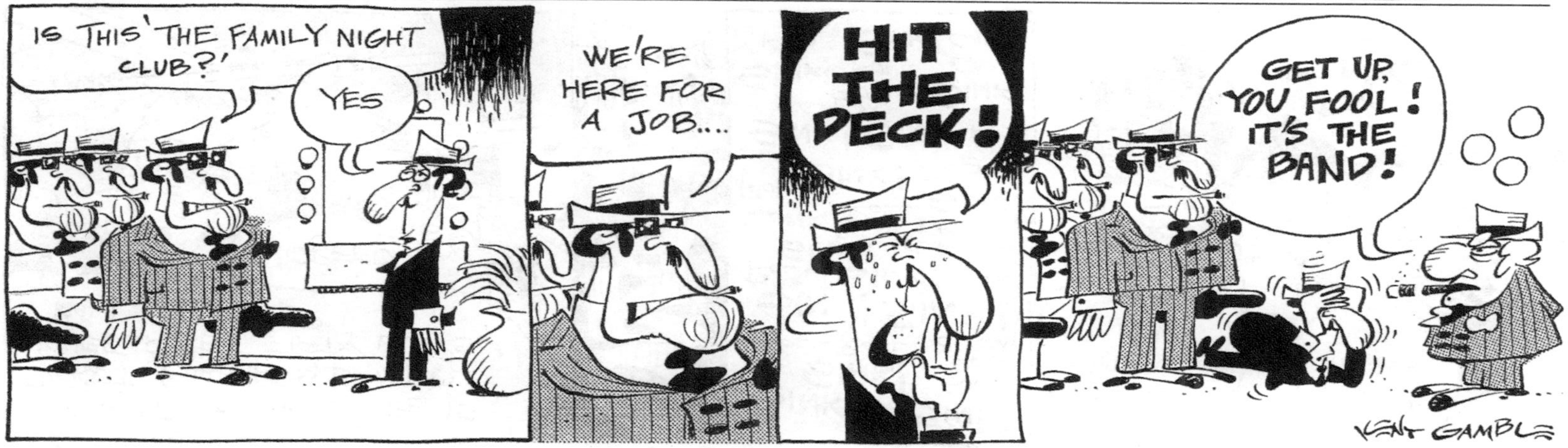
IS THIS 'THE FAMILY NIGHT CLUB?'
YES
WE'RE HERE FOR A JOB....
HIT THE DECK!
GET UP, YOU FOOL! IT'S THE BAND!
KENT GAMBLE

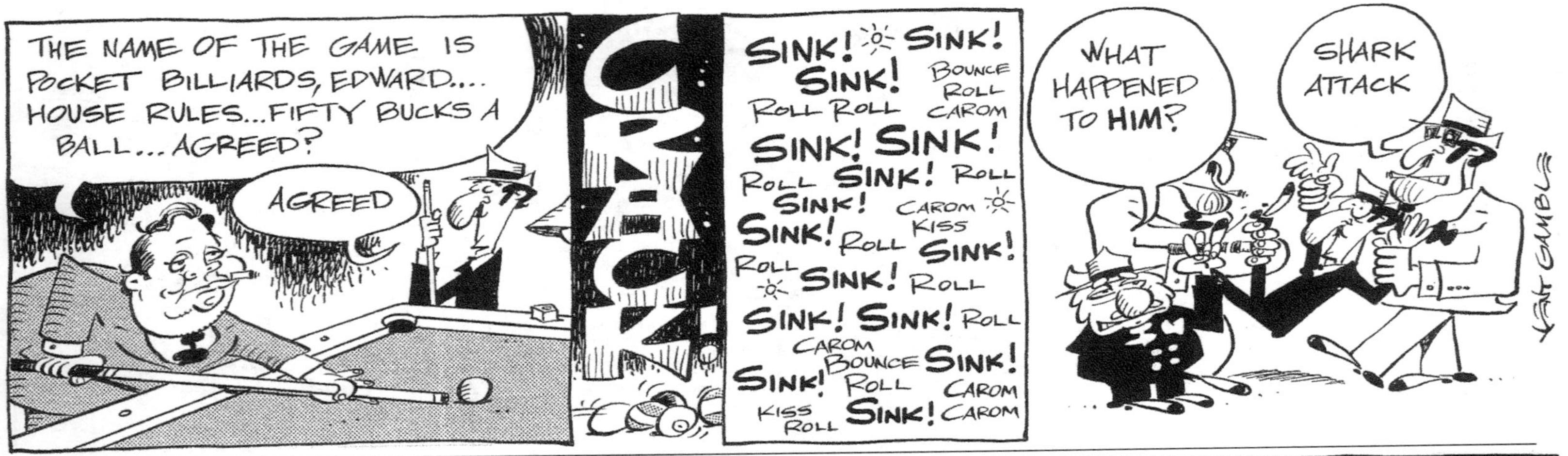
THE NAME OF THE GAME IS POCKET BILLIARDS, EDWARD... HOUSE RULES...FIFTY BUCKS A BALL... AGREED?
AGREED
CRACK!
SINK! SINK! SINK! BOUNCE ROLL ROLL ROLL CAROM SINK! SINK! ROLL SINK! ROLL SINK! CAROM KISS SINK! ROLL SINK! ROLL SINK! ROLL SINK! SINK! ROLL CAROM BOUNCE SINK! SINK! ROLL CAROM KISS ROLL SINK! CAROM
WHAT HAPPENED TO HIM?
SHARK ATTACK

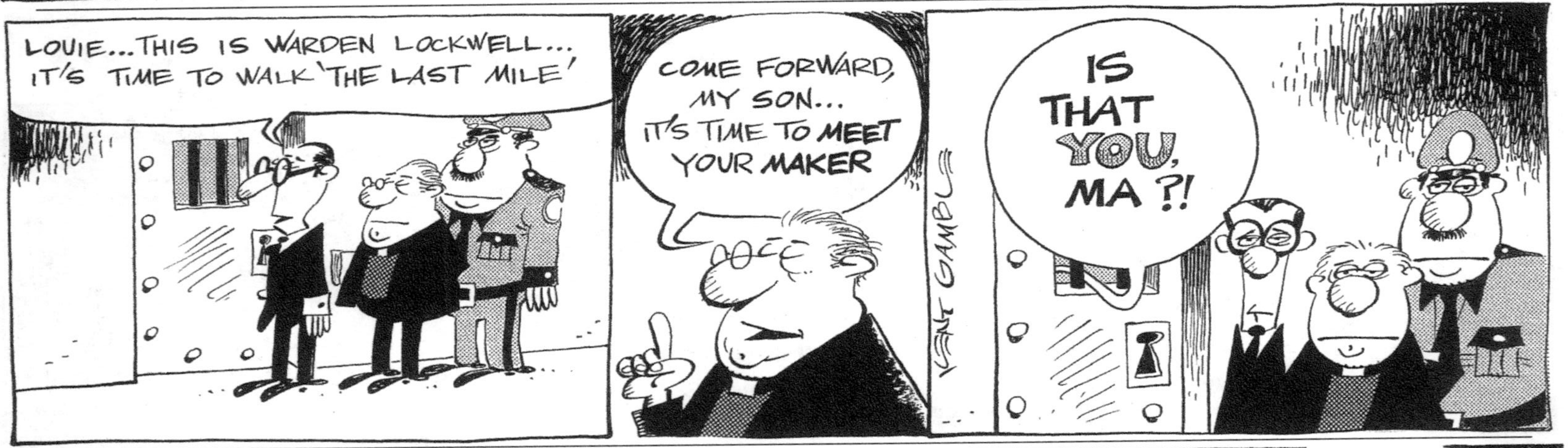
LOUIE...THIS IS WARDEN LOCKWELL... IT'S TIME TO WALK 'THE LAST MILE'
COME FORWARD, MY SON... IT'S TIME TO MEET YOUR MAKER
IS THAT YOU, MA ?!

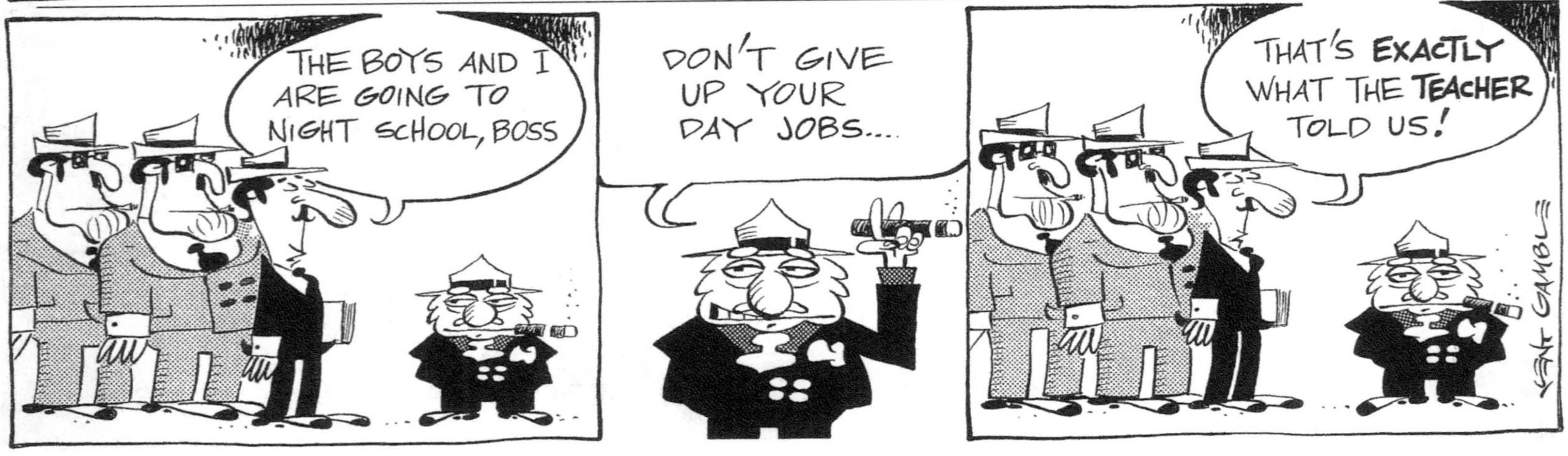
THE BOYS AND I ARE GOING TO NIGHT SCHOOL, BOSS
DON'T GIVE UP YOUR DAY JOBS...
THAT'S EXACTLY WHAT THE TEACHER TOLD US!

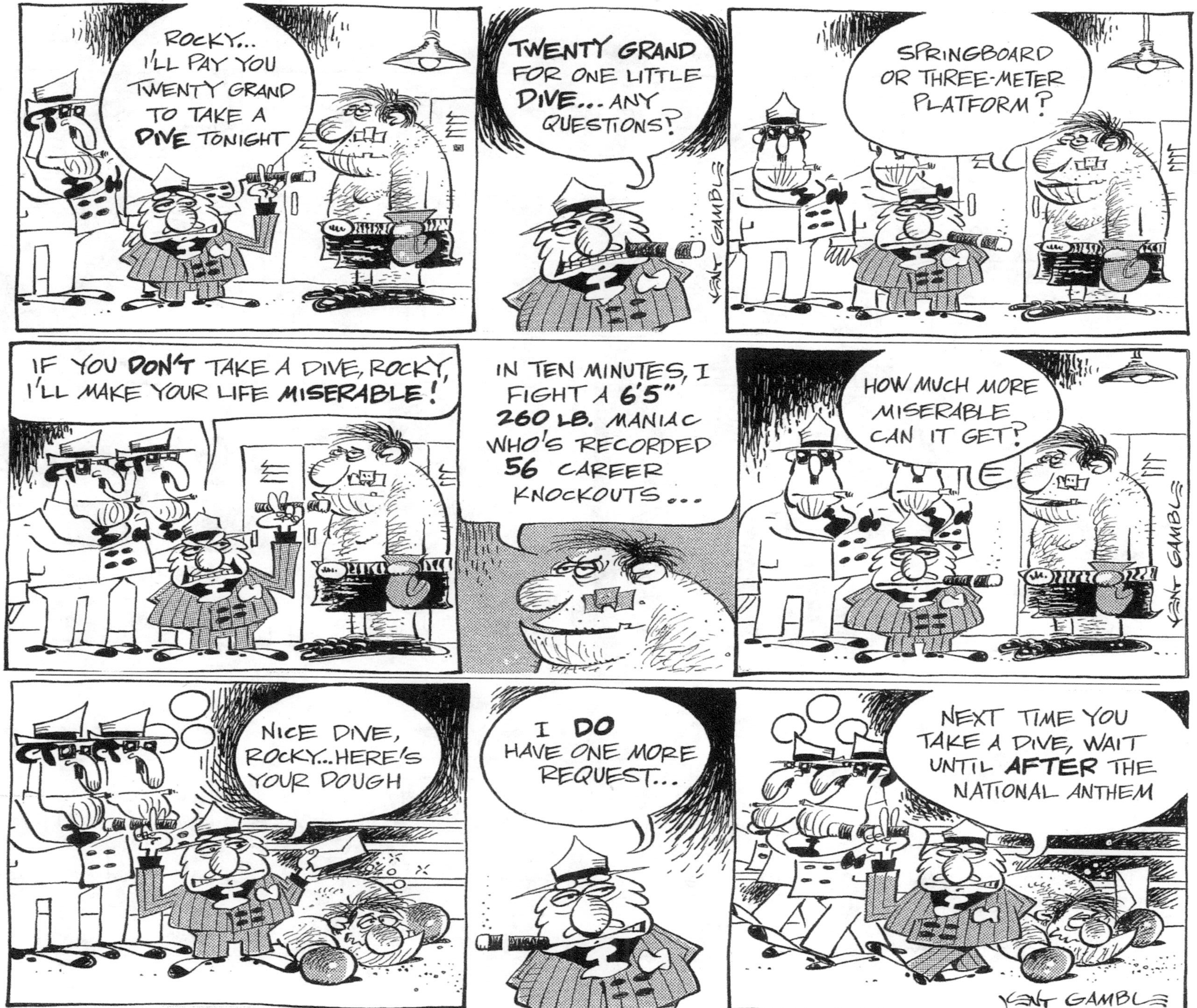
ROCKY... I'LL PAY YOU TWENTY GRAND TO TAKE A DIVE TONIGHT
TWENTY GRAND FOR ONE LITTLE DIVE... ANY QUESTIONS?
KENT GAMBLE
SPRINGBOARD OR THREE-METER PLATFORM?
IF YOU DON'T TAKE A DIVE, ROCKY, I'LL MAKE YOUR LIFE MISERABLE!
IN TEN MINUTES, I FIGHT A 6'5" 260 LB. MANIAC WHO'S RECORDED 56 CAREER KNOCKOUTS...
HOW MUCH MORE MISERABLE CAN IT GET?
KENT GAMBLE
NICE DIVE, ROCKY... HERE'S YOUR DOUGH
I DO HAVE ONE MORE REQUEST...
NEXT TIME YOU TAKE A DIVE, WAIT UNTIL AFTER THE NATIONAL ANTHEM
KENT GAMBLE

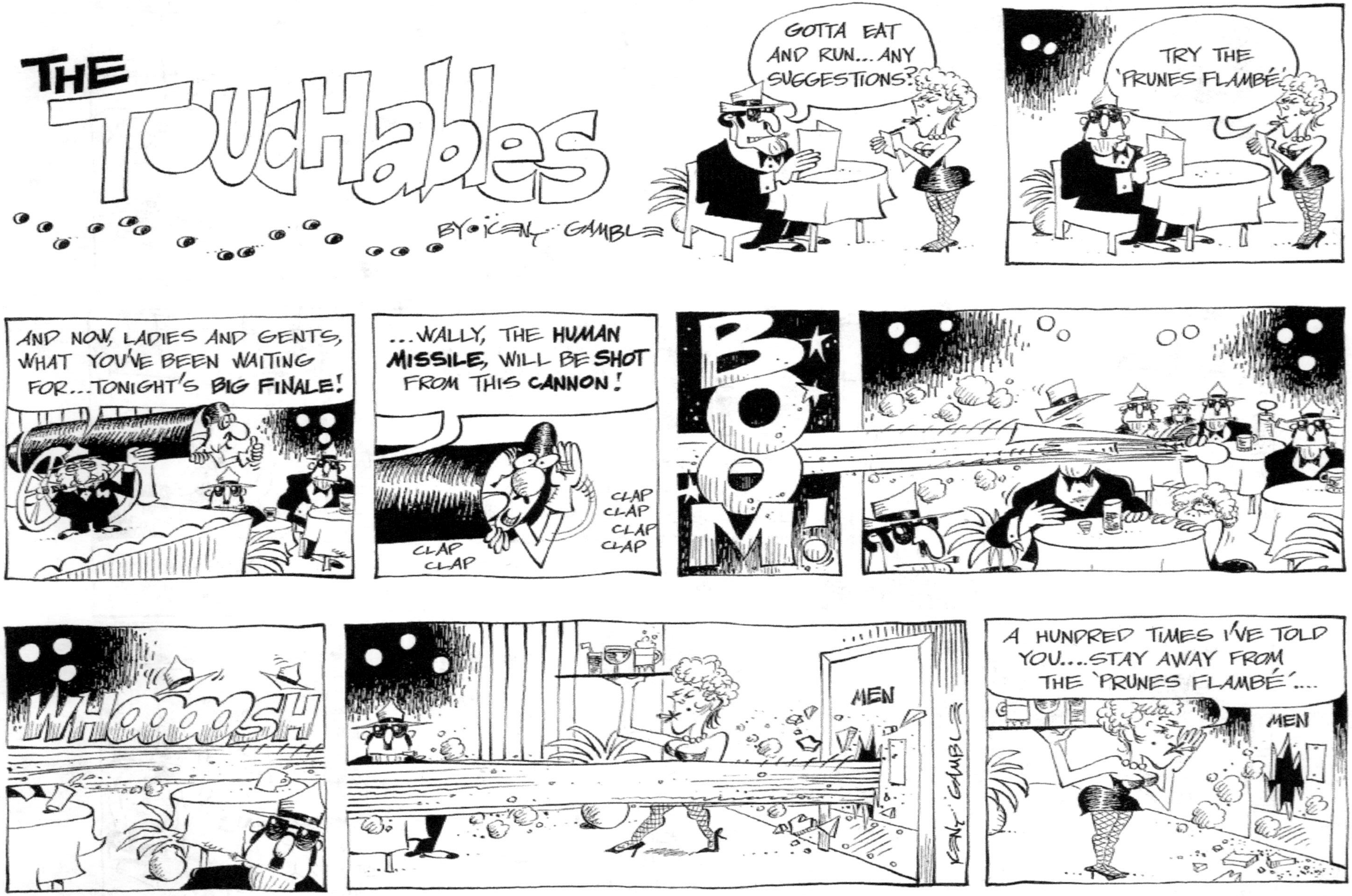
THE TOUCHABLES
BY KEN GAMBLE
GOTTA EAT AND RUN... ANY SUGGESTIONS?
TRY THE 'PRUNES FLAMBÉ'
AND NOW, LADIES AND GENTS, WHAT YOU'VE BEEN WAITING FOR... TONIGHT'S BIG FINALE!
...WALLY, THE HUMAN MISSILE, WILL BE SHOT FROM THIS CANNON!
CLAP CLAP
CLAP CLAP CLAP CLAP
BOOM!
WHOOOOSH
MEN
KEN GAMBLE
A HUNDRED TIMES I'VE TOLD YOU....STAY AWAY FROM THE 'PRUNES FLAMBÉ'....
MEN

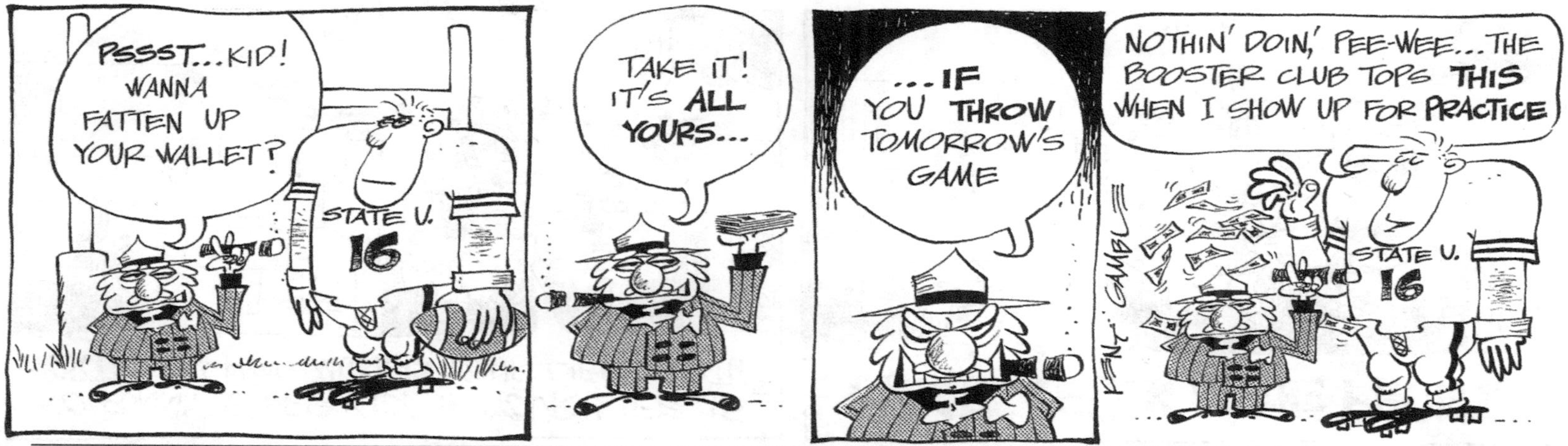
PSSST...KID! WANNA FATTEN UP YOUR WALLET?
STATE U. 16
TAKE IT! IT'S ALL YOURS...
...IF YOU THROW TOMORROW'S GAME
NOTHIN' DOIN,' PEE-WEE...THE BOOSTER CLUB TOPS THIS WHEN I SHOW UP FOR PRACTICE
STATE U. 16
KENT GAMBLE

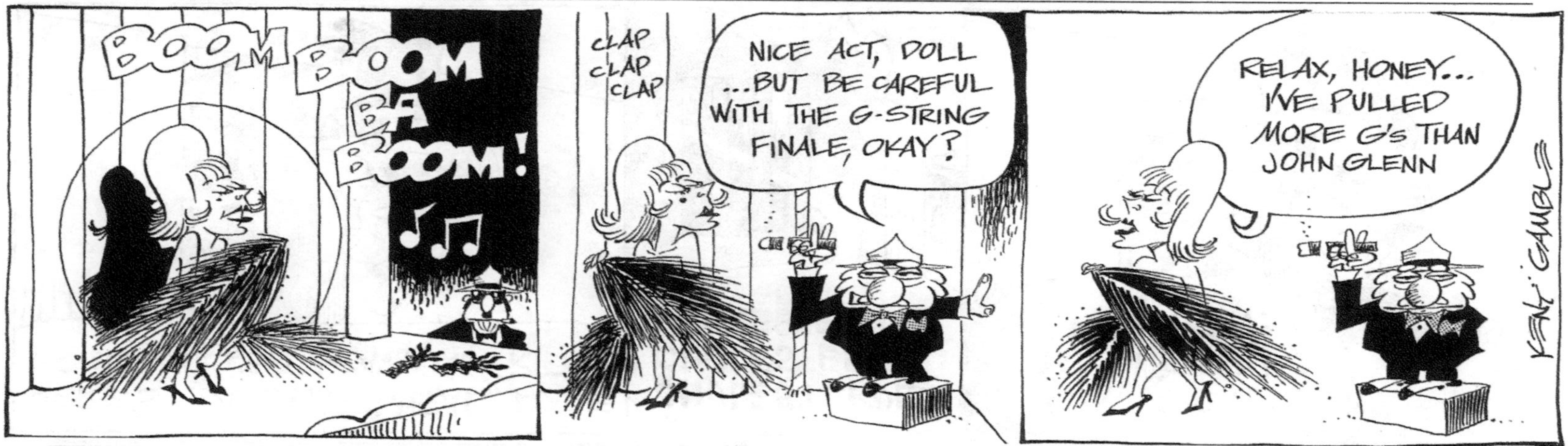
BOOM BOOM BA BOOM!
CLAP CLAP CLAP
NICE ACT, DOLL ...BUT BE CAREFUL WITH THE G-STRING FINALE, OKAY?
RELAX, HONEY... I'VE PULLED MORE G's THAN JOHN GLENN
KENT GAMBLE

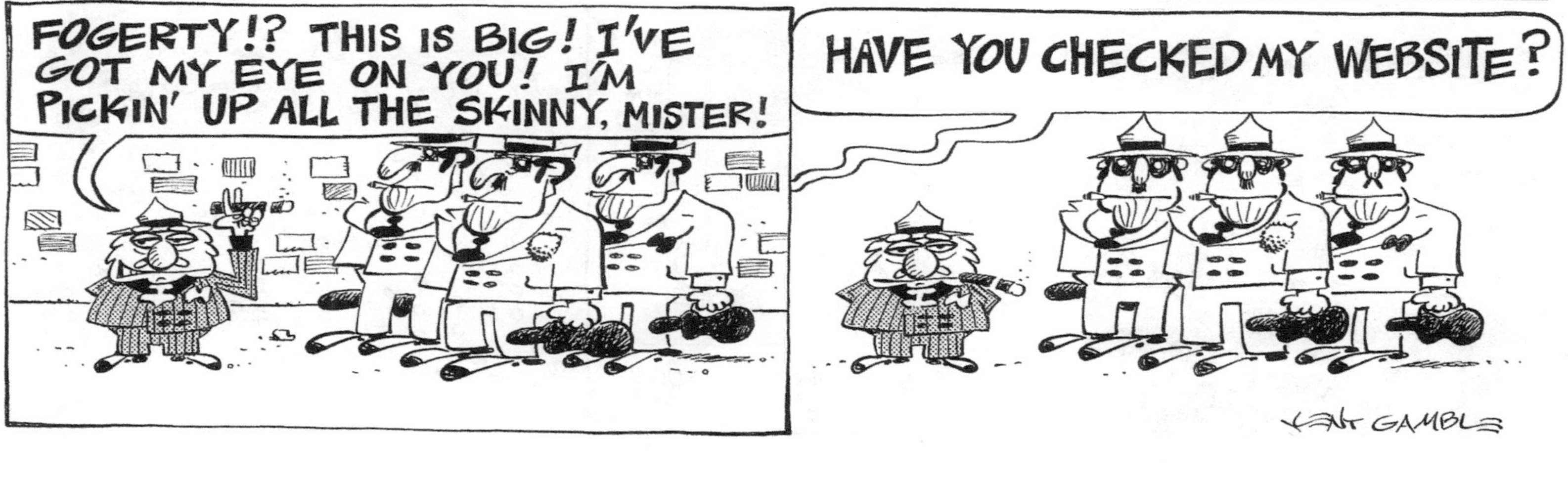
FOGERTY!? THIS IS BIG! I'VE GOT MY EYE ON YOU! I'M PICKIN' UP ALL THE SKINNY, MISTER!
HAVE YOU CHECKED MY WEBSITE?
KENT GAMBLE

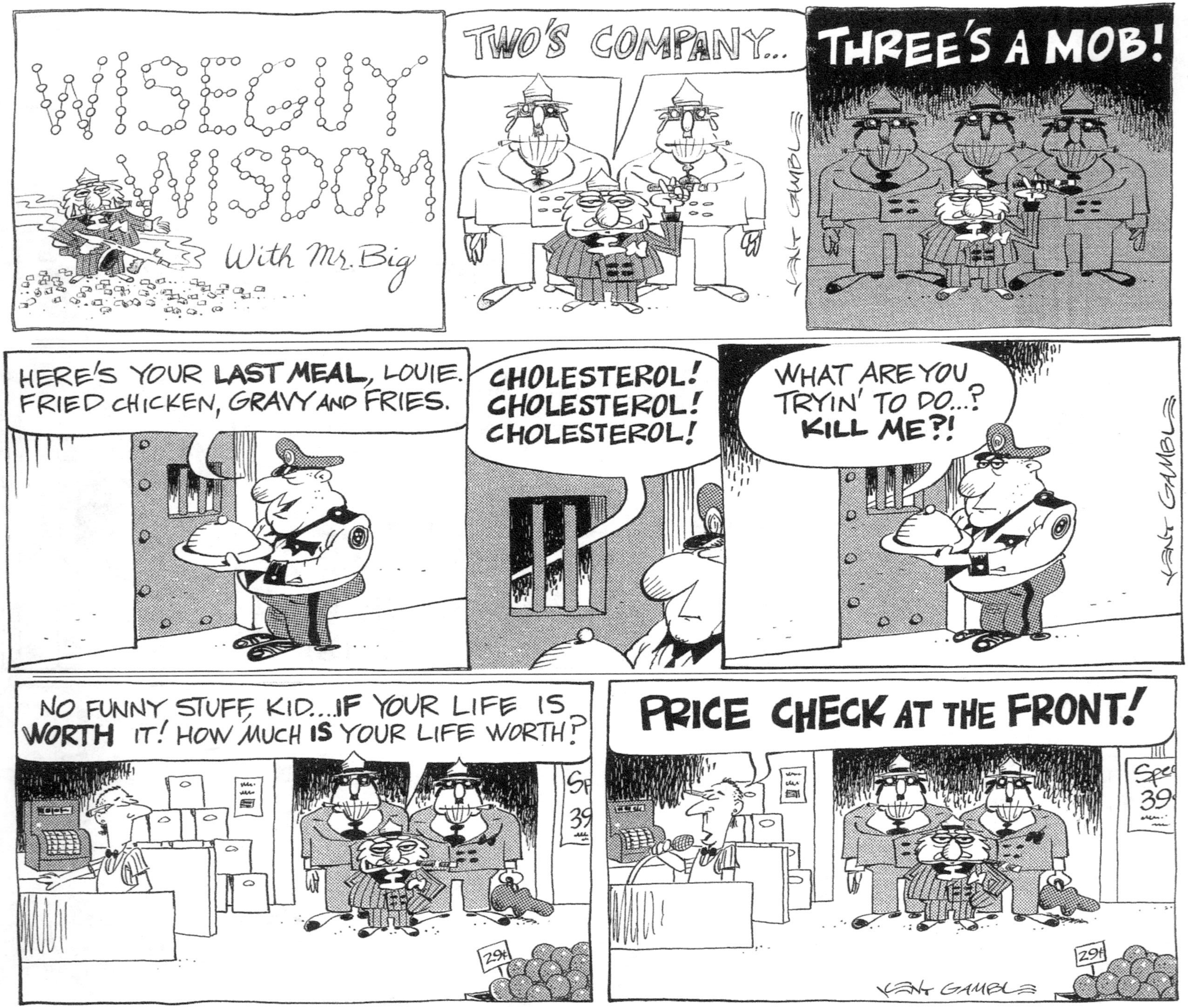
WISEGUY WISDOM
With Mr. Big
TWO'S COMPANY...
THREE'S A MOB!
Kent Gamble
HERE'S YOUR LAST MEAL, LOUIE. FRIED CHICKEN, GRAVY AND FRIES.
CHOLESTEROL! CHOLESTEROL! CHOLESTEROL!
WHAT ARE YOU TRYIN' TO DO...? KILL ME?!
Kent Gamble
NO FUNNY STUFF, KID...IF YOUR LIFE IS WORTH IT! HOW MUCH IS YOUR LIFE WORTH?
29¢
PRICE CHECK AT THE FRONT!
29¢
Kent Gamble

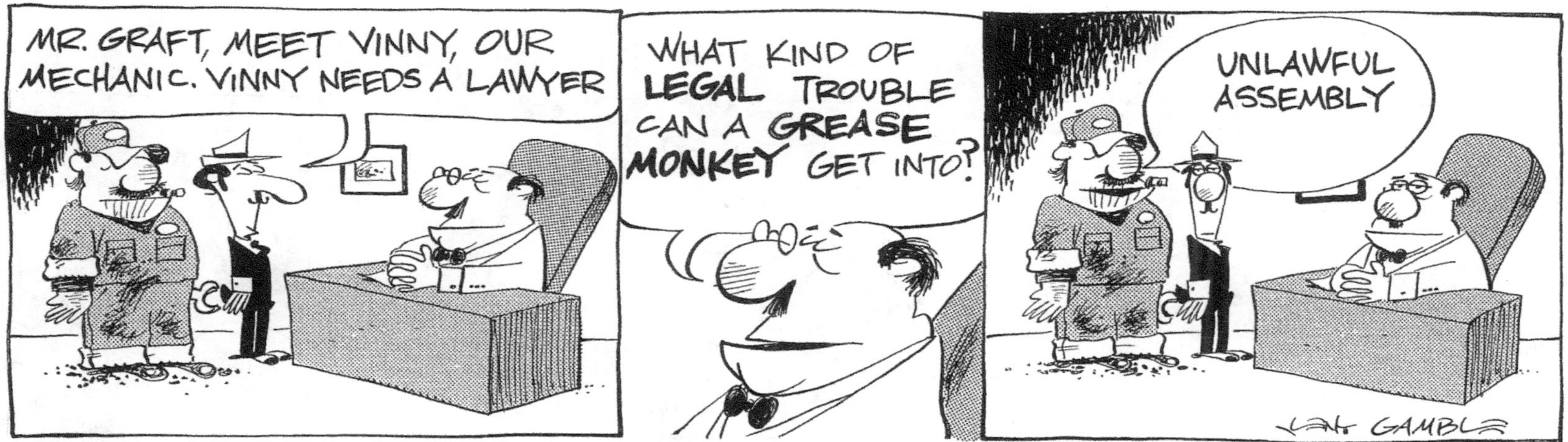
MR. GRAFT, MEET VINNY, OUR MECHANIC. VINNY NEEDS A LAWYER
WHAT KIND OF **LEGAL** TROUBLE CAN A **GREASE MONKEY** GET INTO?
UNLAWFUL ASSEMBLY
KENT GAMBLE

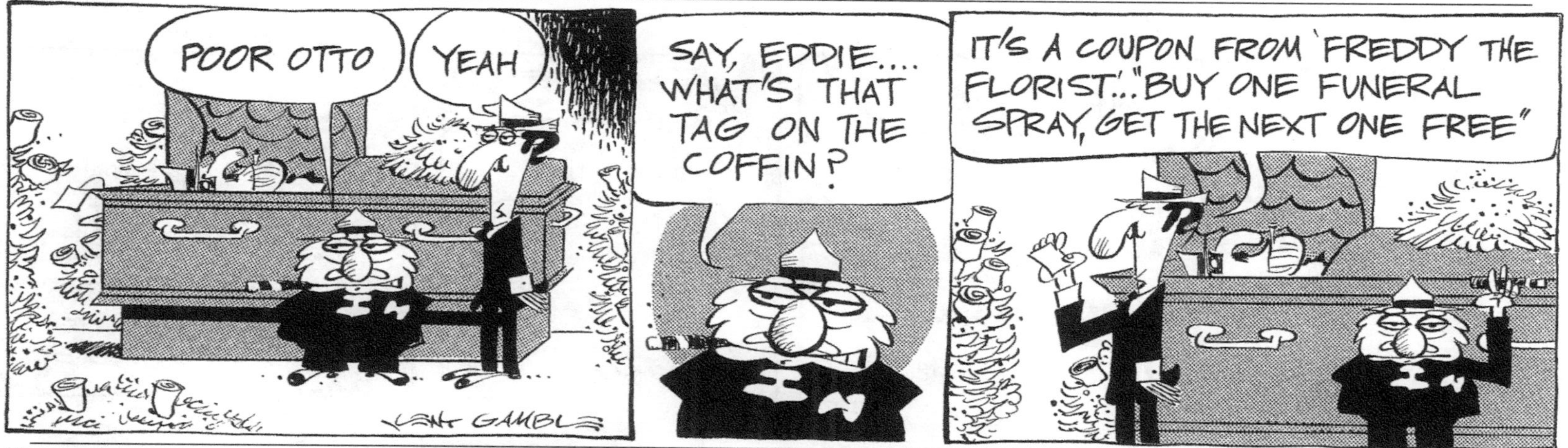
POOR OTTO
YEAH
KENT GAMBLE
SAY, EDDIE.... WHAT'S THAT TAG ON THE COFFIN?
IT'S A COUPON FROM 'FREDDY THE FLORIST'..."BUY ONE FUNERAL SPRAY, GET THE NEXT ONE FREE"

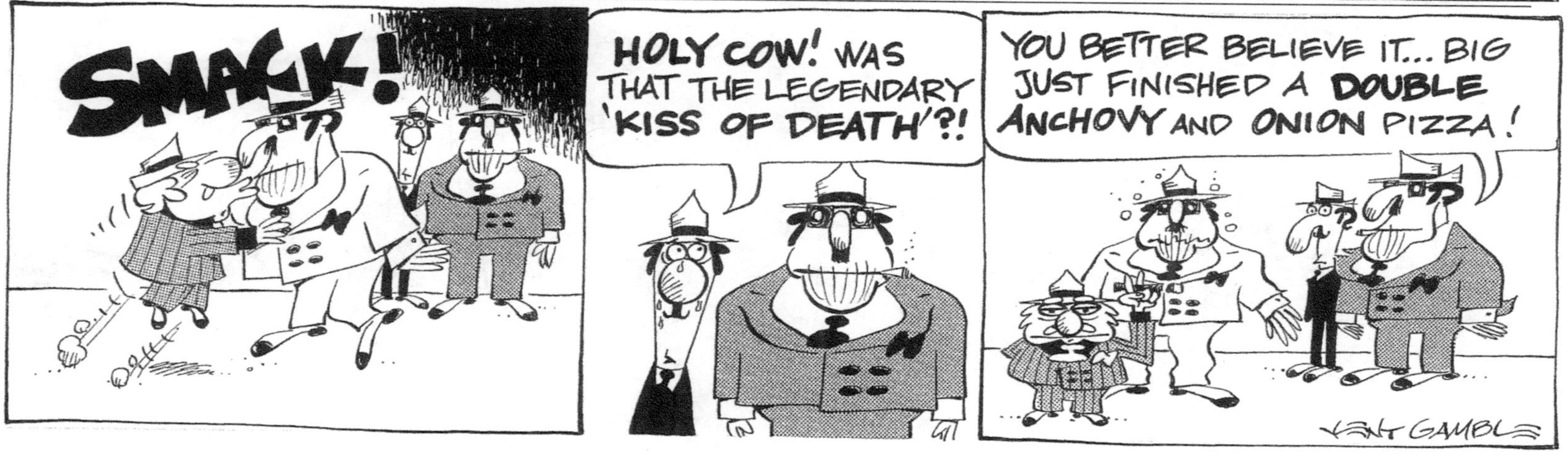
SMACK!
HOLY COW! WAS THAT THE LEGENDARY '**KISS OF DEATH**'?!
YOU BETTER BELIEVE IT... BIG JUST FINISHED A **DOUBLE ANCHOVY** AND **ONION** PIZZA!
KENT GAMBLE

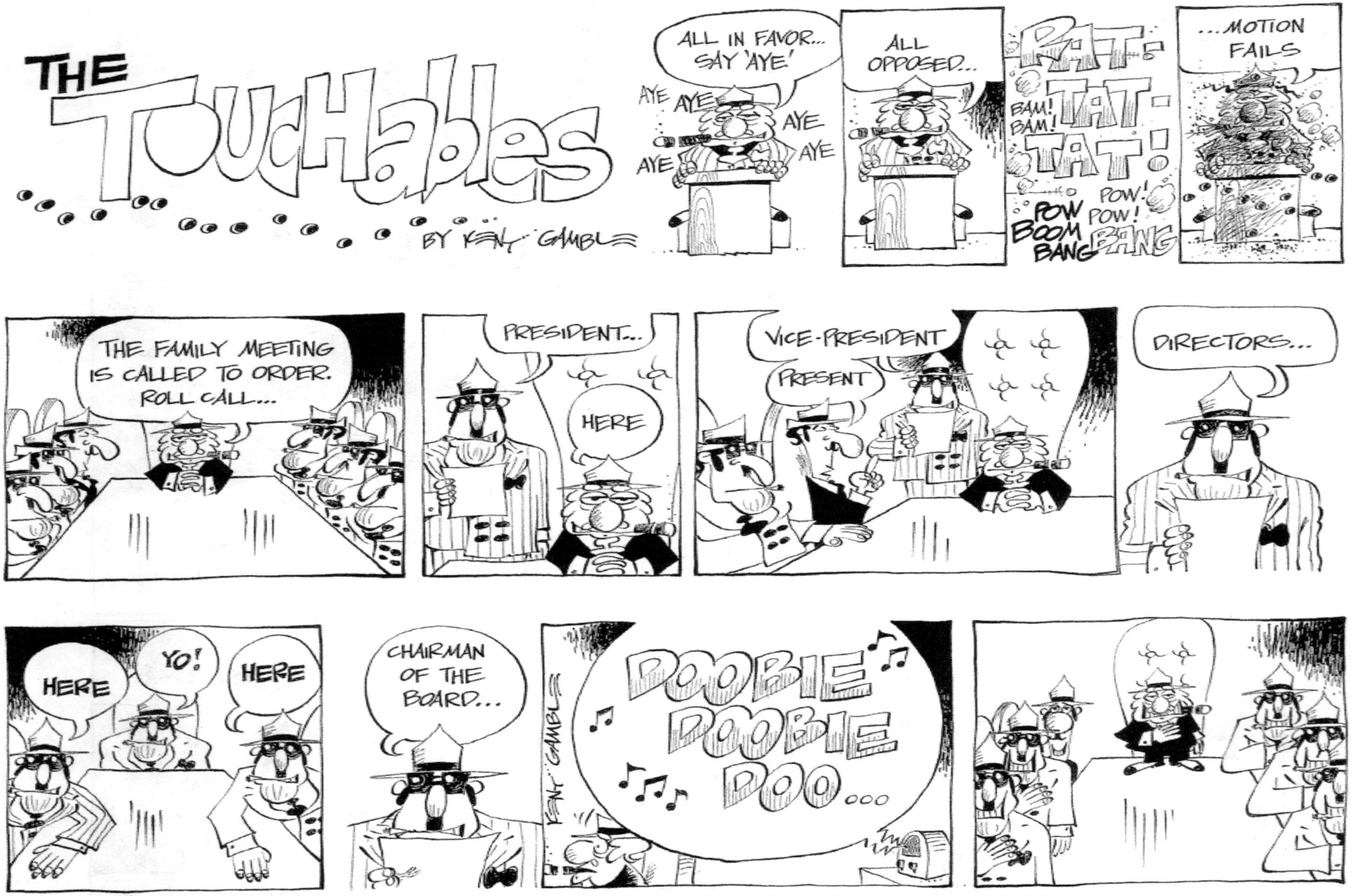
THE TOUCHABLES
BY KEN GAMBLE
THE FAMILY MEETING IS CALLED TO ORDER. ROLL CALL...
PRESIDENT...
HERE
VICE-PRESIDENT
PRESENT
DIRECTORS...
HERE
YO!
HERE
CHAIRMAN OF THE BOARD...
KEN GAMBLE
DOOBIE DOOBIE DOO...
ALL IN FAVOR... SAY 'AYE'
AYE AYE
AYE
AYE
AYE
ALL OPPOSED...
RAT-TAT-TAT!
BAM! BAM!
POW BOOM BANG
POW! POW! BANG
...MOTION FAILS

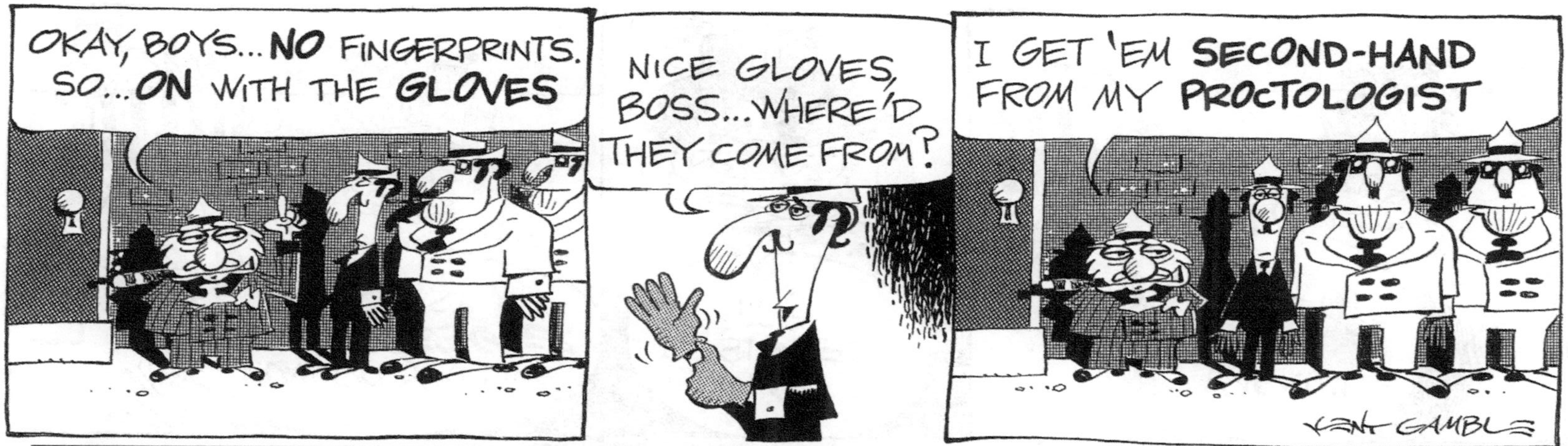
OKAY, BOYS... NO FINGERPRINTS. SO... ON WITH THE GLOVES
NICE GLOVES, BOSS... WHERE'D THEY COME FROM?
I GET 'EM SECOND-HAND FROM MY PROCTOLOGIST
KENT GAMBLE

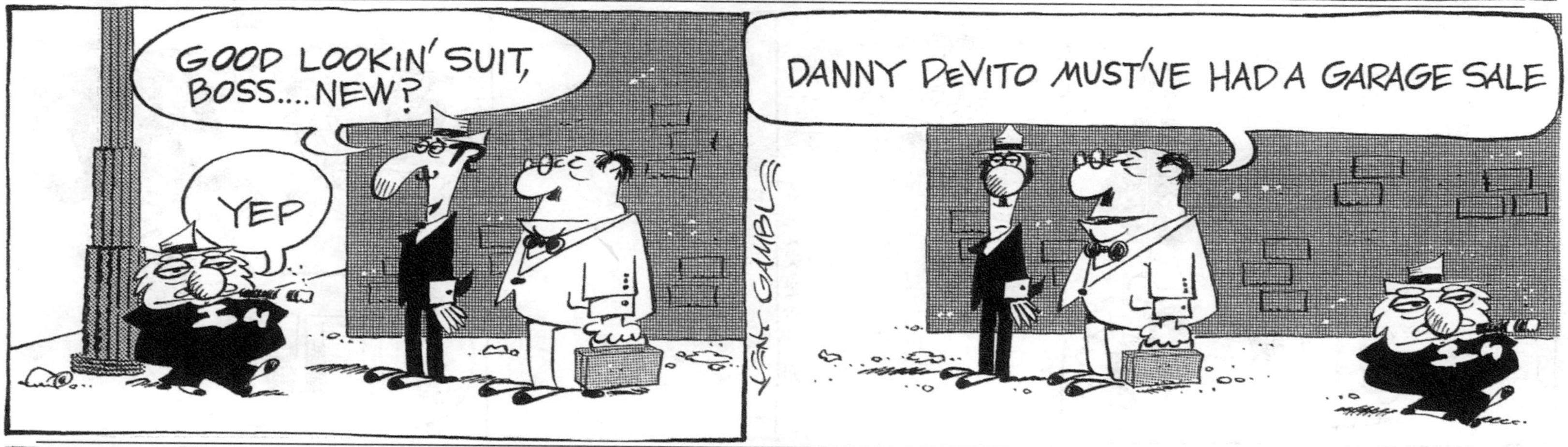
GOOD LOOKIN' SUIT, BOSS.... NEW?
YEP
KENT GAMBLE
DANNY DeVITO MUST'VE HAD A GARAGE SALE

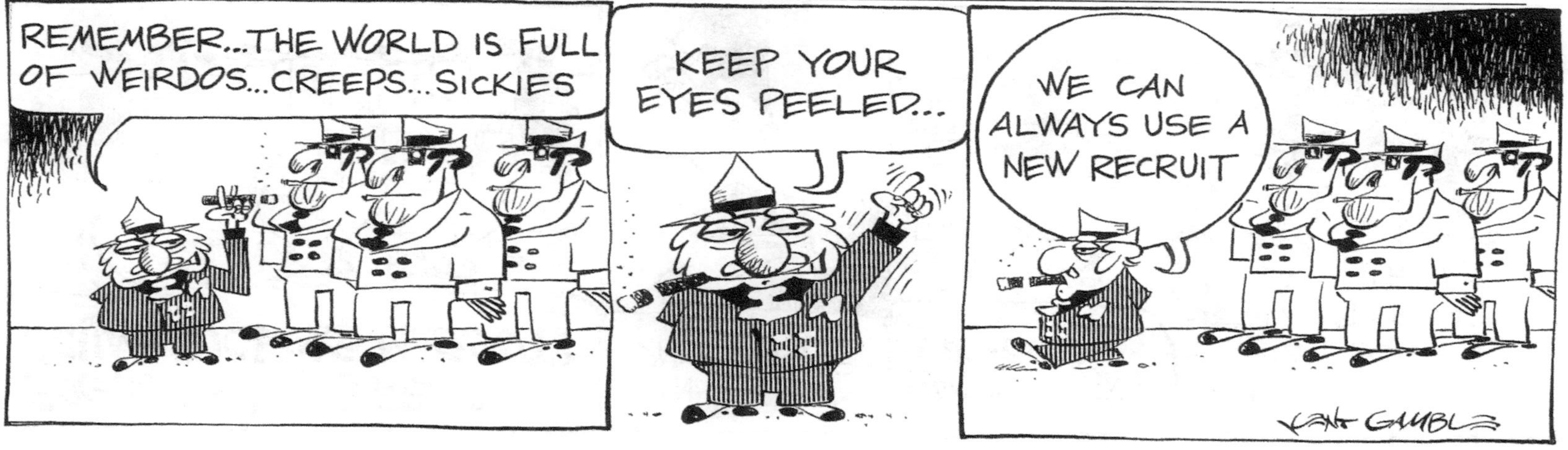
REMEMBER... THE WORLD IS FULL OF WEIRDOS... CREEPS... SICKIES
KEEP YOUR EYES PEELED...
WE CAN ALWAYS USE A NEW RECRUIT
KENT GAMBLE

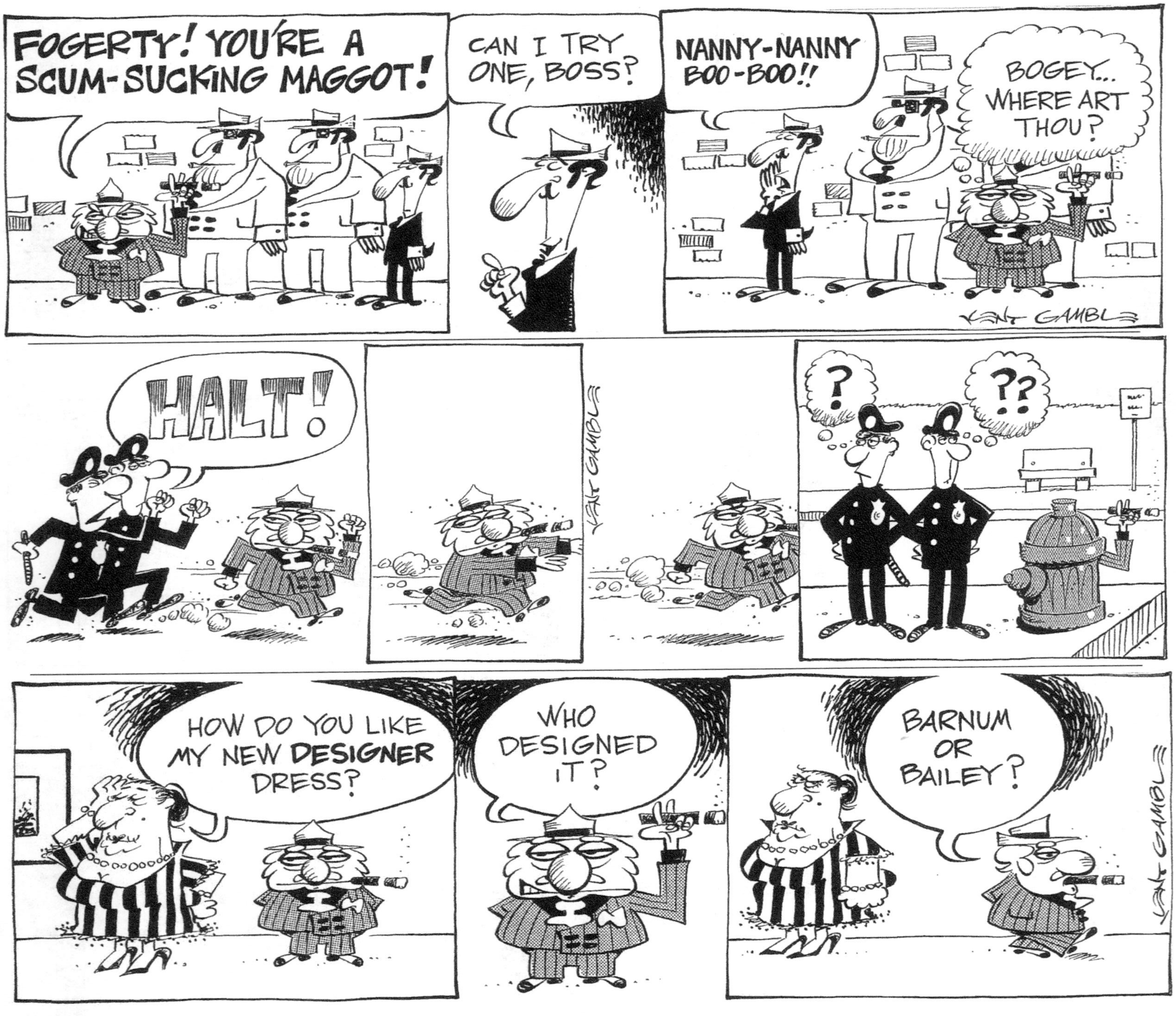
FOGERTY! YOU'RE A SCUM-SUCKING MAGGOT!
CAN I TRY ONE, BOSS?
NANNY-NANNY BOO-BOO!!
BOGEY... WHERE ART THOU?
HALT!
?
??
HOW DO YOU LIKE MY NEW DESIGNER DRESS?
WHO DESIGNED IT?
BARNUM OR BAILEY?

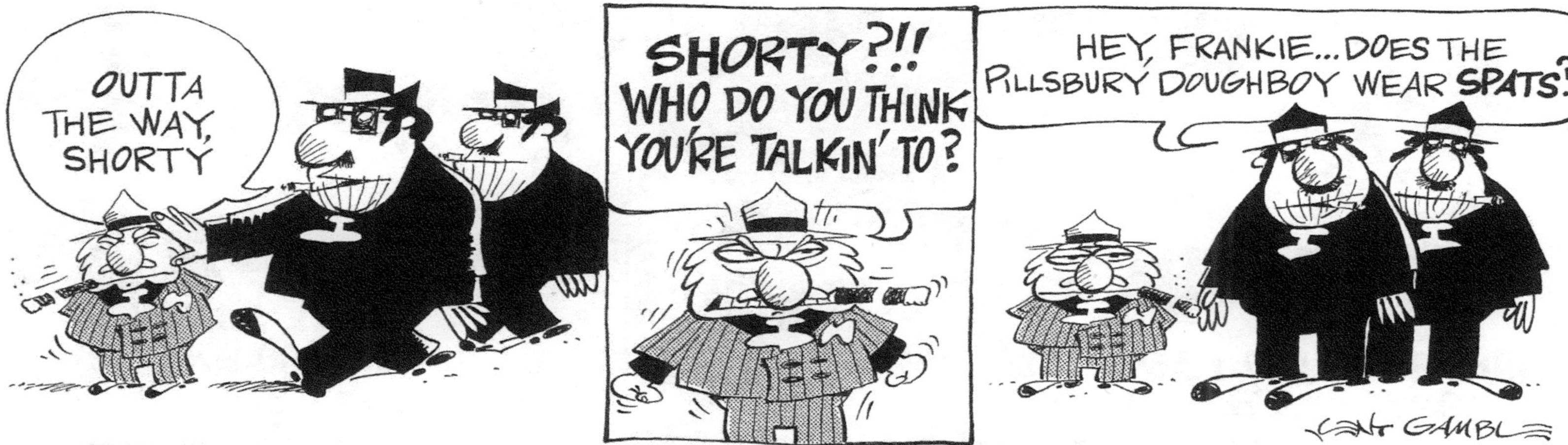
OUTTA THE WAY, SHORTY
SHORTY?!! WHO DO YOU THINK YOU'RE TALKIN' TO?
HEY, FRANKIE... DOES THE PILLSBURY DOUGHBOY WEAR SPATS?
KENT GAMBLE

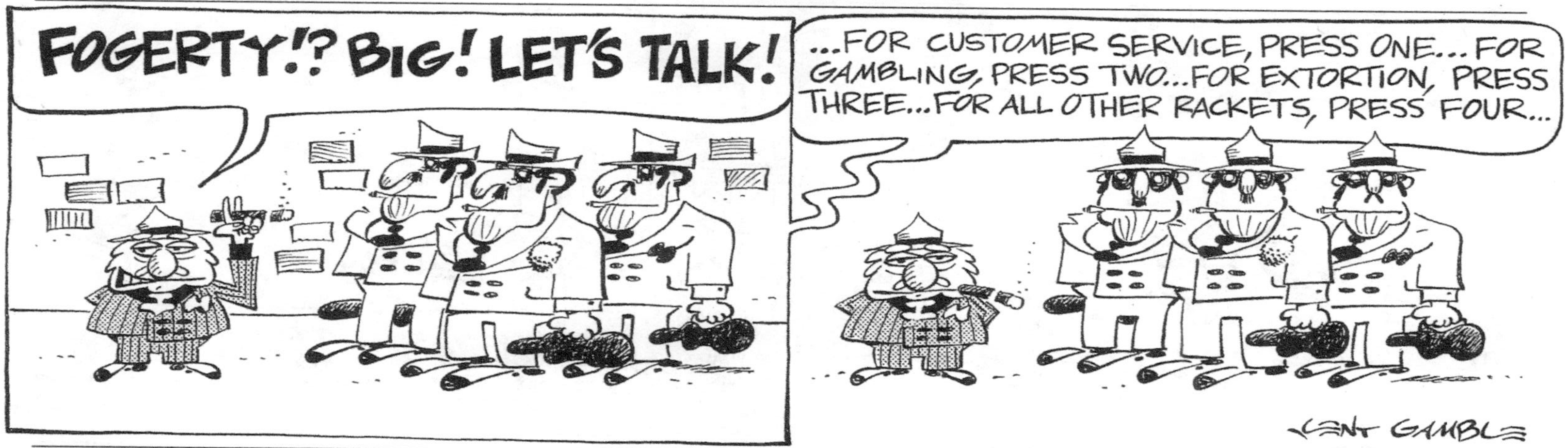
FOGERTY!? BIG! LET'S TALK!
...FOR CUSTOMER SERVICE, PRESS ONE... FOR GAMBLING, PRESS TWO...FOR EXTORTION, PRESS THREE...FOR ALL OTHER RACKETS, PRESS FOUR...
KENT GAMBLE

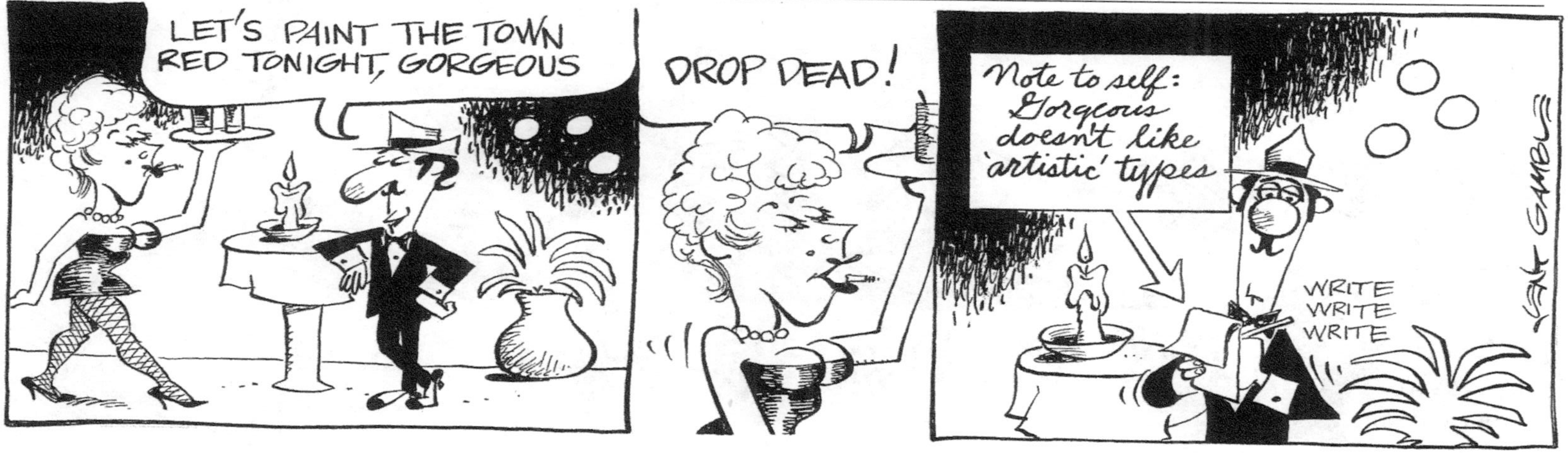
LET'S PAINT THE TOWN RED TONIGHT, GORGEOUS
DROP DEAD!
Note to self: Gorgeous doesn't like 'artistic' types
WRITE WRITE WRITE
KENT GAMBLE

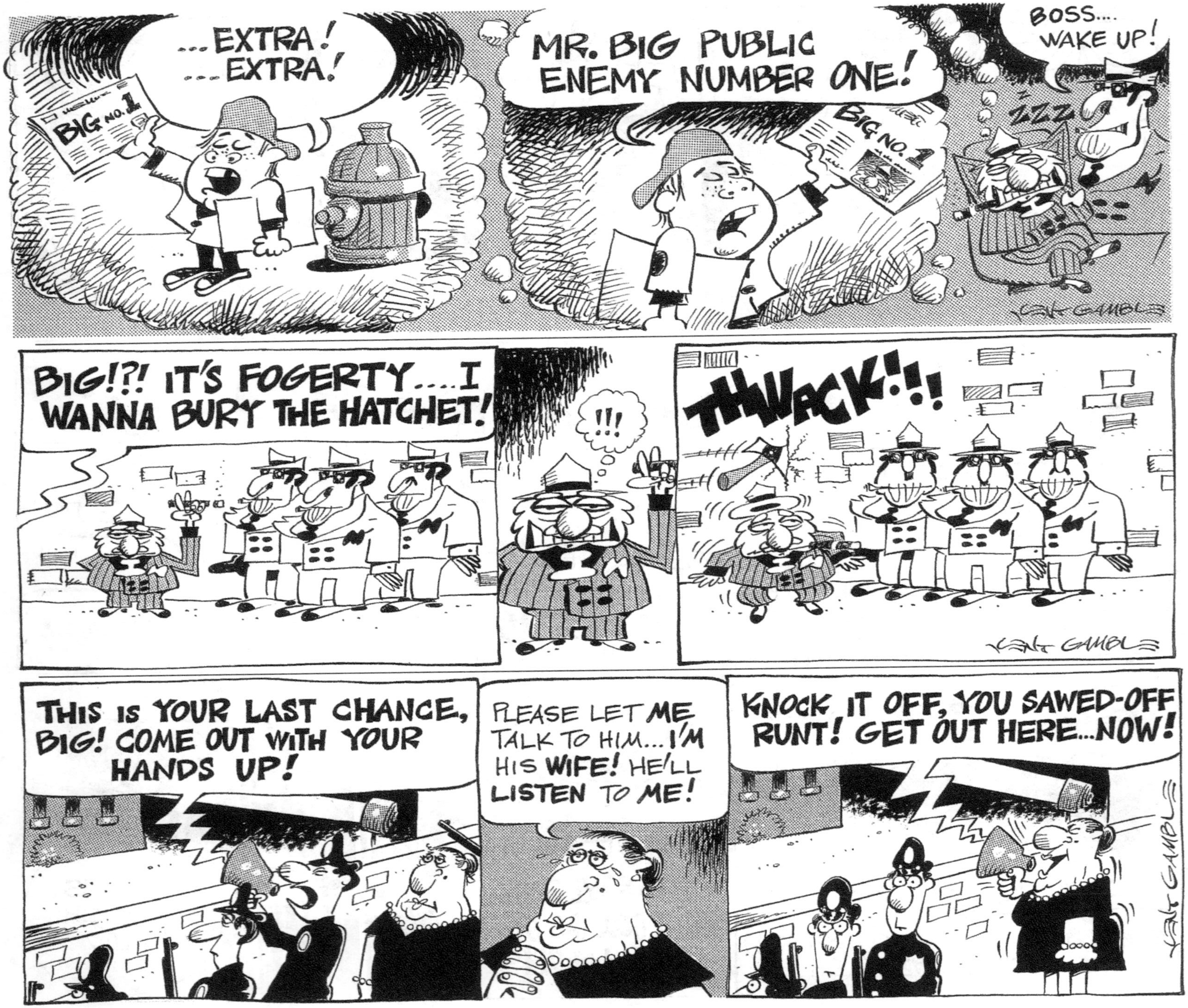
...EXTRA! ...EXTRA!
BIG NO. 1
MR. BIG PUBLIC ENEMY NUMBER ONE!
BIG NO. 1
BOSS.... WAKE UP!
ZZZ
BIG!?! IT'S FOGERTY.... I WANNA BURY THE HATCHET!
!!!
THWACK!!!
THIS IS YOUR LAST CHANCE, BIG! COME OUT WITH YOUR HANDS UP!
PLEASE LET ME TALK TO HIM... I'M HIS WIFE! HE'LL LISTEN TO ME!
KNOCK IT OFF, YOU SAWED-OFF RUNT! GET OUT HERE...NOW!
KENT GAMBLE

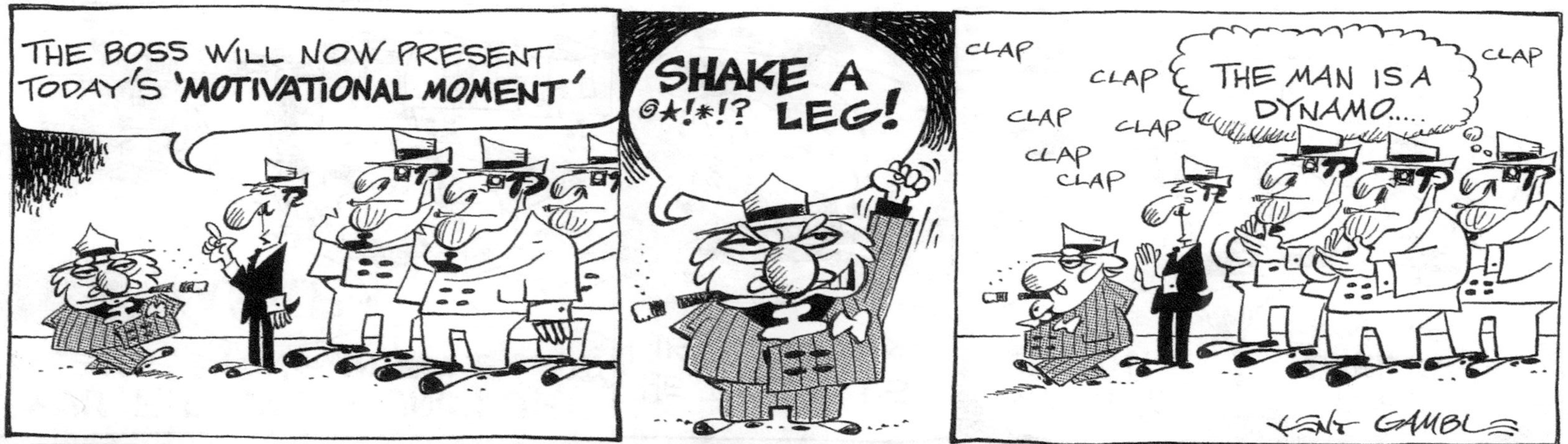
THE BOSS WILL NOW PRESENT TODAY'S 'MOTIVATIONAL MOMENT'
SHAKE A @★!*!? LEG!
CLAP CLAP CLAP CLAP CLAP CLAP CLAP
THE MAN IS A DYNAMO.....
KENT GAMBLE

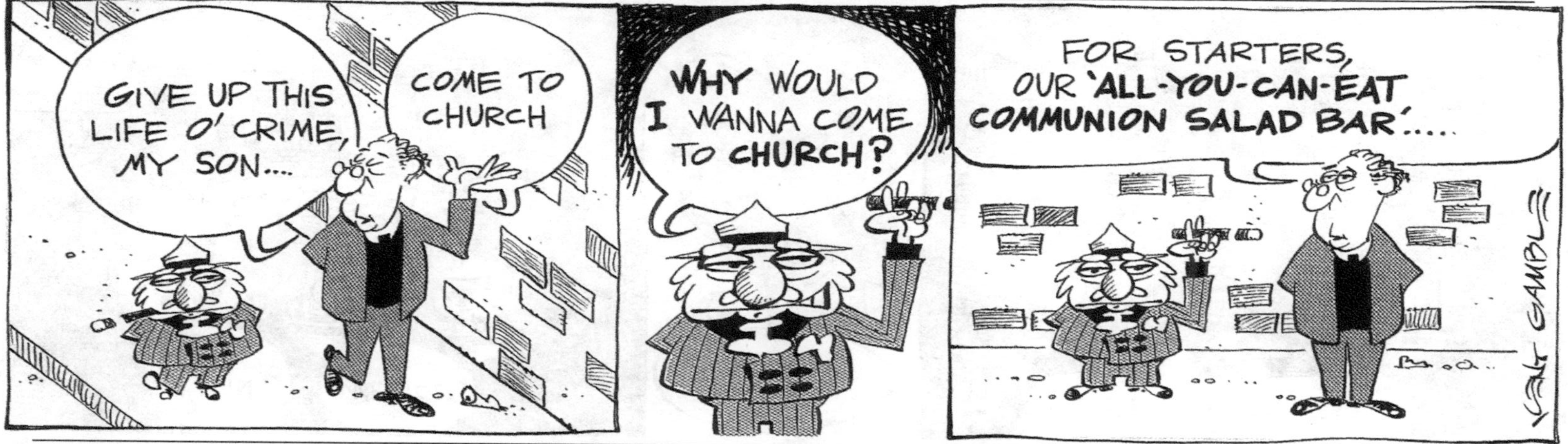
GIVE UP THIS LIFE O' CRIME, MY SON....
COME TO CHURCH
WHY WOULD I WANNA COME TO CHURCH?
FOR STARTERS, OUR 'ALL-YOU-CAN-EAT COMMUNION SALAD BAR'.....
KENT GAMBLE

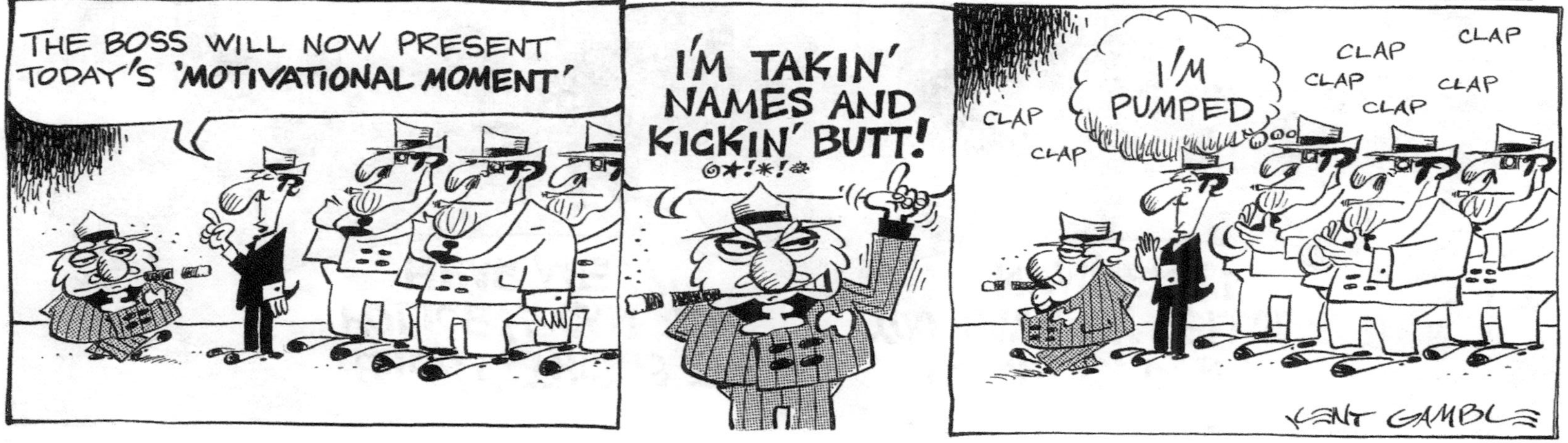
THE BOSS WILL NOW PRESENT TODAY'S 'MOTIVATIONAL MOMENT'
I'M TAKIN' NAMES AND KICKIN' BUTT! @★!*!
I'M PUMPED
CLAP CLAP CLAP CLAP CLAP CLAP CLAP
KENT GAMBLE

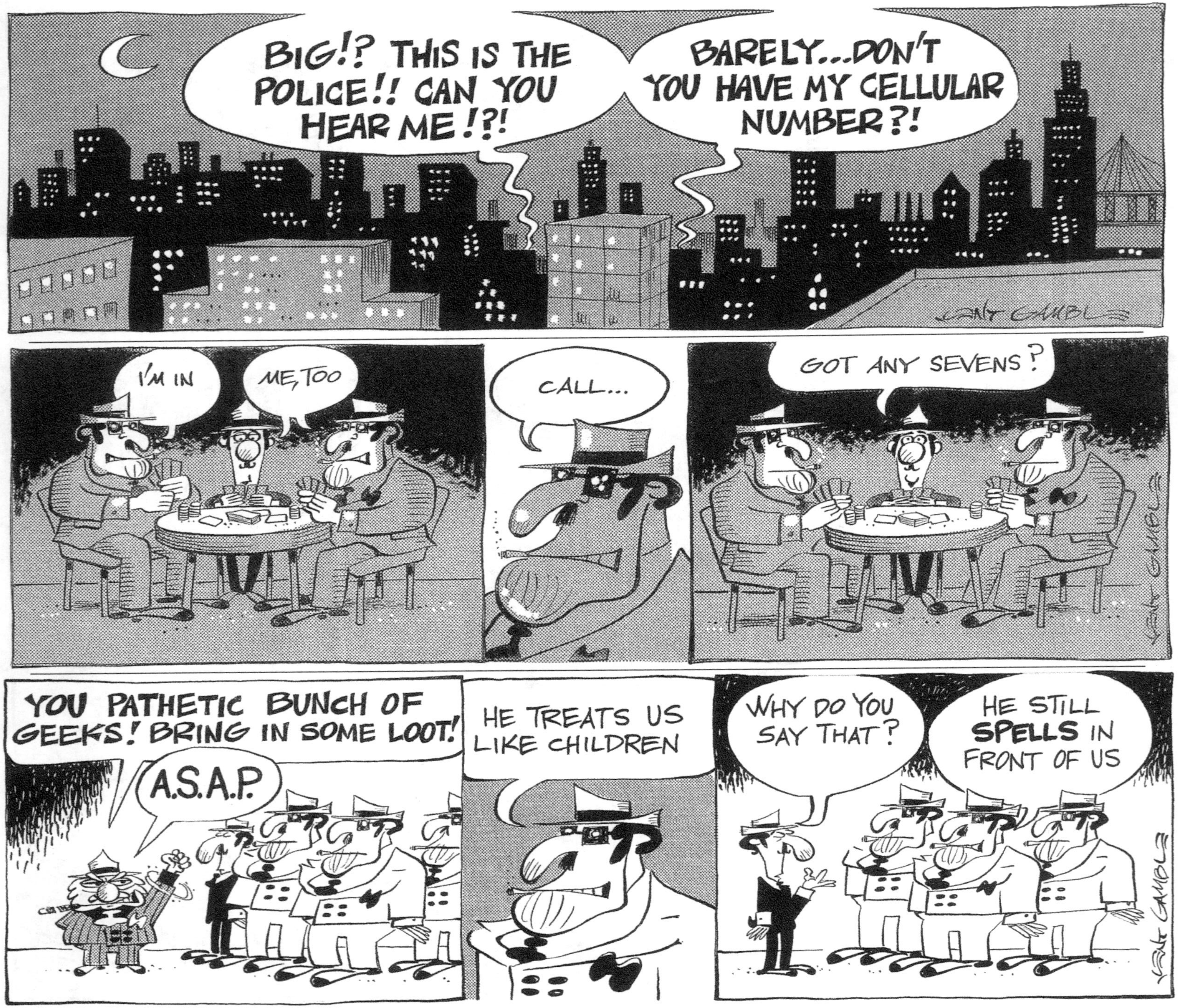
BIG!? THIS IS THE POLICE!! CAN YOU HEAR ME!?!
BARELY...DON'T YOU HAVE MY CELLULAR NUMBER?!
I'M IN
ME, TOO
CALL...
GOT ANY SEVENS?
YOU PATHETIC BUNCH OF GEEKS! BRING IN SOME LOOT!
A.S.A.P.
HE TREATS US LIKE CHILDREN
WHY DO YOU SAY THAT?
HE STILL SPELLS IN FRONT OF US

KENT GAMBLE

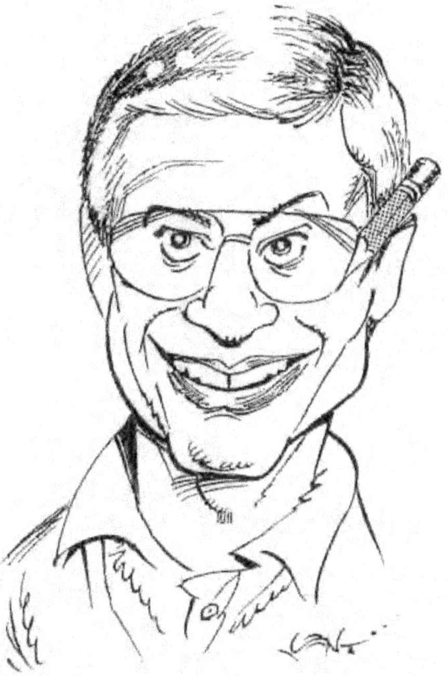
KENT

ARTIST/WRITER

A WAYWARD CARTOONIST
LOOKING FOR A GOOD
PUNCHLINE

Kent Gamble, cartoonist for magazines such as *Cracked* and *Crazy*, provides his comic strip collection of *"The Touchables"* which is about a bumbling gang of mobsters led by Mr. Big and joined by Fast Eddie and "the boys". The biggest problem Mr. Big faces though is not the other mob gangs but the terror (to him) that is Mrs. Big. Includes both the Sundays and the daily strips.

In addition to *Cracked* and *Crazy,* Kent is the artist for the series of books written by Len Berman, *"And Nobody got Hurt!"* which featurs the weirdest and wackiest true sport stories. Kent has also illustrated a number of Texas themed books including: *Rave On; Read My Lips; and Til the Fat Lady Sings.*

He is currently working on some original cartoon illustrations for a few Binary Publication titles set to appear in 2013.

Binary
PUBLICATIONS

A new line of books centered around art, pop culture, and glamour.

Launched in late 2012, be sure to check out the website for updates on current and future titles.

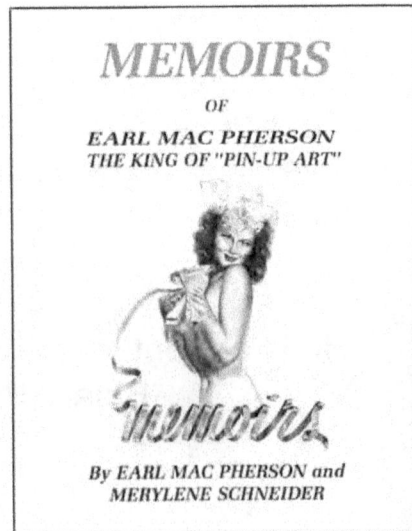

www.ingramcontent.com/pod-product-compliance
Lightning Source LLC
Chambersburg PA
CBHW080529030426
42337CB00023B/4672